# How They Became Famous Dancers

## A Dancing History

### Anne Dunkin

Cover Design and Book Layout
Jonathan Cashatt

Illustrations
Christy Little

# Contents

# Introduction

How do you become a famous dancer? This history tells the story of six women and six men who did exactly that. Their lives spanned the seventeenth into the twenty-first centuries. They were born in different parts of the world: France, Hungary, India, Japan, Mexico, Russia, Sweden, Trinidad, and the United States. And their physical appearances display a variety of physical sizes, body shapes, and skin colors.

Each had his/her own personality traits and background experiences. Some of them were born into wealthy families with performing arts contacts. Others were born poor with no arts contacts. Some studied dance with the best teachers of the time. Others studied with whomever they found, and two were self-taught. Several had strong family ties while others had no such support. Some even left their homelands to dance. Each found different reasons—as well as different ways—to dance. Some perfected dance techniques from the past, some embellished dancing they saw around them every day, and some created dancing that was totally new. But now forever linked in time, they all shared one important thing, a passion for dancing. Once discovered, each pursued that passion to success.

History answers questions by showing us paths that others have taken. Following those footsteps we become detectives. We get to decide where to look for pieces of the puzzle. There are secondary sources prepared by others who have already written about our subject. But seeking new details requires digging deeper for primary sources. Perhaps our subject kept a journal or wrote an autobiography. Maybe there are painted portraits, photographs, films or videos to view. There may even be family members or associates to contact. There is much to explore.

Writing this history about the lives of famous dancers has been a special treat because I like detective work, I love dancing, and I had wonderful collaborators who gave their time and suggestions to help. There were dance educators and historians: Arvin Ajona, Karen Bradley, Mary Alice "Buff" Brennan, Theresa Purcell Cone, Mary-Jean Cowell, Anne Green Gilbert, Juliana Macke, Elsa Posey, and Patricia Reedy. There were also associates who worked directly with the subjects: Ann Hutchinson Guest, Peggy and Murray Schwartz, Anthony Shay, and Judy Tyrus; and family members Michelle Ito and Charles Woodford.

Once the words were assembled, the talents of others turned them into the text you are about to read. First, Jonathan Cashatt's creativity, expertise, and patience designed, formatted, and directed the publishing process. Then Christy Little provided illustrations to enhance the dancers' individual stories, and David Cashatt detailed source and image citations. And finally throughout the entire project, Brad Willis, my husband and life partner, gave unwavering support. He is my objective sounding board, tireless editor, and enthusiastic cheer leader. With admiration, deepest appreciation and gratitude I thank you all.

Now, as reader, you become part of *How They Became Famous Dancers: A Dancing History.*

*In loving memory for our friend,*
*Karin Vartowski,*
*the creative dancer within us all.*

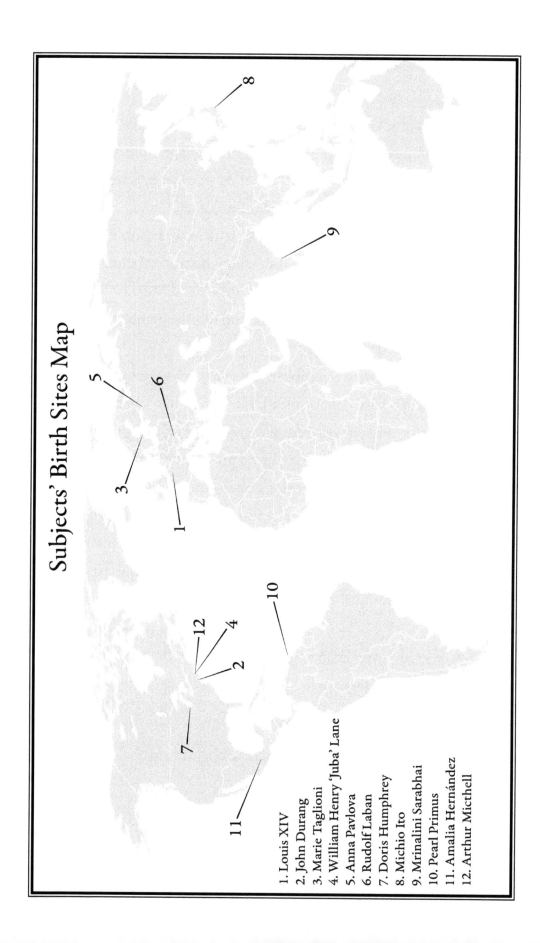

# Subjects' Birth Sites Map

1. Louis XIV
2. John Durang
3. Marie Taglioni
4. William Henry 'Juba' Lane
5. Anna Pavlova
6. Rudolf Laban
7. Doris Humphrey
8. Michio Ito
9. Mrinalini Sarabhai
10. Pearl Primus
11. Amalia Hernández
12. Arthur Micthell

# Louis XIV
## 1638-1715

This story begins with King Louis XIV of France who loved to dance. Choosing the sun as his symbol, Louis called himself the 'Sun King' as he ruled France for seventy-two years from 1643-1715. Many people described his reign as a glorious time for France. They thought his life was exactly what the life of a king should be.

# Dancing Sun King

France held an important place in the world when Louis was born. Located in Western Europe, it sat next to several countries including Germany, Spain, and Italy. Its borders also touched major bodies of water. The Mediterranean Sea was on the south. To the north were the English Channel and the North Sea. The Rhine River was on the east and the Atlantic ocean was on the west. Access to these bodies of water helped France travel to many parts of the world where it set up trading posts and established colonies.

Louis was the first child of King Louis XIII and Queen Anne of Austria. He had one brother, Philippe, who was two years younger. There were no sisters. But Louis was never alone because there were always servants, courtiers, and family members close by. Louis was just four and a half years old when his father, the king, died. Therefore as the eldest son, Louis became King of France at five years of age. Since he was too young to run the government, his mother, Queen Anne, and Cardinal Mazarin, the Prime Minister, managed it for him.

In the seventeenth century children were expected to behave like adults. They also dressed like adults. Men and boys wore long stockings or hose on their legs. Pants called breeches came to their knees or just above. Their coats were also knee length with voluminous sleeves. Very young boys wore dresses or gowns like Philippe is wearing in the portrait with his older brother Louis. Women and girls wore dresses with tight bodices and floor length skirts over many crinolines.

BORN: September 5, 1638 at Saint-Germain-en-Laye outside Paris, France
DIED: September 1, 1715 at Versailles, France

Children and adults both wore shoes or boots with two-to-three-inch high heels and jeweled buckles. In fact, as an adult, Louis often wore heels up to five inches tall because he was shorter than average height. Everyone had wigs for different occasions and hats of various sizes. Many were large brimmed with feathers. At the royal palace clothing was fancy and rich. Garments made from expensive fabrics and fur were decorated with lace, ruffles, and jewels.

Servants and private tutors educated Louis and Philippe. They learned martial skills, fencing, and horsemanship. They studied geography, history, and other subjects using special decks of cards. The lessons were printed on one side of the cards and the other side was used for playing card games.

In addition to playing cards the boys had windup toys, hobbyhorses, board games and checkers for fun. In the afternoons Louis liked to go outdoors. He went hunting, rode one of his horses, or took a horse and carriage ride through the palace gardens. From an early age he also liked military spectacle. His father had given him a set of solid silver toy soldiers to play with to prepare for his life as a military commander.

One of Louis's favorite activities was dancing. As both social events and as performances, dancing was popular at court. Everyone believed it was excellent for their health and physical appearance. Dancers had good posture and walked with authority.

Performances in the royal residencies were called court ballets, and they told stories of historical characters, kings, and queens. They reenacted marriages and births of the royal family, and celebrated events such as winning a war. Dancers portrayed animals, celestial planets, or feelings like love, peace, honor, or grace. Costumes for dance performances were fancier versions of everyday clothes, and the dance steps were similar in both social dancing and ballet performances. The dancers' feet outlined differently shaped patterns on the floor as they traveled across the room. Sometimes they grouped their bodies together to form geometric shapes. There were slow proudly performed movements and also quick light movements. Both men and women danced in the performances.

Louis inherited a love of dancing from his father, and he began performing in the court ballets when he was eight years old. His courtiers took daily dance lessons and appeared in the court performances with him. This was convenient because the dancing master lived at the royal palace. Skilled musicians, dancing masters played a violin to accompany their students as they learned the latest dances, social manners, and how to behave in court. Dancing masters also created the choreography for the court ballets.

From time to time, Louis heard about groups of people who were unhappy with the government. When they created disturbances, Prime Minister Mazarin always settled the discord. One time to show people that order had been restored, Mazarin presented a special ballet, *Le Ballet de la Nuit (The Ballet of Night)*. Fourteen-year-old Louis starred as Apollo, the Sun King.

*Le Ballet de la Nuit* lasted all night, twelve hours long. There was no electricity or gas light, so the performance was lit by candles. With forty-three different scenes of poetry, music, and dancing, the ballet told many stories. There was beautiful scenery and over one hundred lavish costumes, masks, and props. In the last scene, which was performed at the end of the long night, Louis appeared as Apollo, the rising sun. The ballet showed Louis in full control. The audience saw beauty, order, and harmony in their lives.

When Louis was twenty-two years old, he married Marie-Therese of Spain. The next year Prime Minister Mazarin died, and Louis assumed his position as king. He did not replace Mazarin. Rather he decided to make all decisions himself, and became an 'absolute monarch'.

Louis was dignified, charming, hardworking, and self-disciplined. He liked glory, grandeur, and ceremony. He also liked order and routine. For example, every morning several courtiers helped him rise and get dressed. Each one helped the king put on a specific piece of clothing. In the evening the routine was repeated in reverse as the king prepared for bed.

During his life Louis had several homes. His favorite was the Palace of Versailles, a six-hour carriage ride from Paris. Louis spent twenty years building the palace, and when it was finished, he moved his court and the government of France to Versailles. If you divide the layout of the buildings and grounds in half, one half looks like a mirror image of the other. Symmetrical design reflected Louis's love of order and balance.

No expense was spared for building this huge palace. Many large halls were decorated with marble, fine woods, and ivory. One was completely covered with mirrors. Furnishings were upholstered with brocades, satins, fur, and velvets. Jewels, gold, silver, and other precious metals were everywhere. Thirty-seven thousand acres of land surrounded the palace. There were gardens, lakes, parks, forests, and hunting areas. Gardens were filled with tulips, orange trees, fountains, and statues.

Many people lived at the palace. The king's family members had their own private apartments. Courtiers and servants, who worked at the palace, also lived there with their families. Everyone attended mass at the palace chapel. There were several dining halls, and many kitchens to prepare large banquets.

Dogs lived at the palace too. Louis loved his small papillons and placed a gilded kennel for them close to his private bed chamber. This way he could personally feed them every morning and night. His dogs, considered family members, appeared in family portraits.

Throughout his reign, Louis kept his love of dance. Although he stopped performing at age thirty-one, he continued taking classes and producing court ballets and performances three evenings a week. Louis knew the power of keeping his subjects happy and showing them beauty in their lives.

He also knew the power of keeping order among his courtiers. As a result, excellent dancing skill was required to serve at Louis's court. This was in addition to military and other abilities. Courtiers kept busy training, rehearsing, and performing. That way they did not have the time or energy to plot against the king or fight amongst themselves. Poor dancing skill could demote a courtier to serving at an outlying post away from the palace.

In 1661 Louis XIV created the Royal Academy of Dance to improve dance training. Dancing masters recorded rules for teaching and performing ballet. They gave specific names to steps and body positions. Court ballets provided a model for these rules.

In 1672 he established the Royal Academy of Music, which later became the Paris Opera.

In 1701 dance notation was published for people to learn dances of the time. France remained the authority on ballet for almost two hundred years. Today around the world ballet steps are still identified by their French names.

In other matters Louis expanded the boundaries of France and led his army in battle when needed. He extended the reign of France to include posts along the coast of Africa, and settlements in the West Indies and in Canada. In America the French settled the area between the Mississippi River and the Rocky Mountains. Reaching from Canada to the Gulf of Mexico, the area was named Louisiana after Louis. French influence spread to many parts of the world and its culture and fashion ruled Europe for years. French dancing masters accompanied French traders and settlers traveling around the world.

Louis died at age seventy-seven in 1715. He had fourteen children and outlived most of them. His great-grandson Louis XV became King at his death. Like his great-grandfather, Louis XV was only five years old when he became King of France.

## Create A Dance

Raoul Auger Feuillet, a dancing master and choreographer, published a notation system for dance during the reign of Louis XIV. On the next page is a sheet of Feuillet's notation for you to read.

**Three rules for ballet performance established by Louis XIV's Royal Academy of Dance included keeping a straight back with erect posture, turning legs out at the hip, and using rounded arms moving from the center of the body outward.**

## *Dancing at Louis's Court*
### Warm up

- Stand with your back straight. Place heels together. Open your toes to the sides away from your heels. Your feet should now look like one corner of a square.
- Take four steps forward with your feet and legs turned out. Stop.
- Round your arms like you are holding a large ball in front of you. Open your arms out to the sides. Lower them keeping the rounded shape.
- Walk four more steps with your back straight, your legs turned out, and your arms rounded.

Now you are ready to join Louis and his guests in
the large hall at the Palace of Versailles.

# The Dance

At the bottom of the page are arrows to show you where to begin.

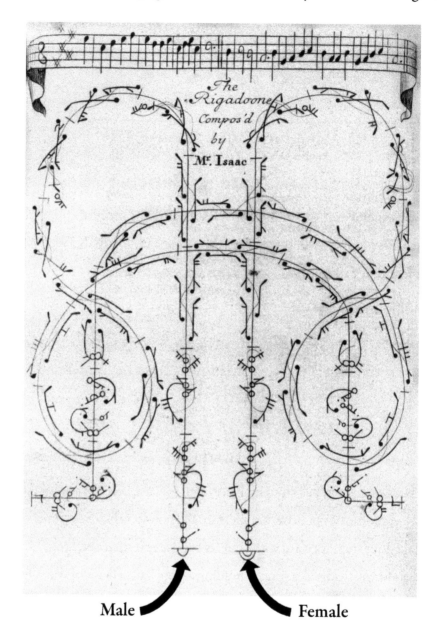

Male           Female

- Bow to your partner. Following your straight and curved path you have eighteen steps to its end.

This is the way Louis liked to dance. How do you like it?

# John Durang
## 1768-1822

The first American-born professional dancer was John Durang. Always curious and asking questions, John may have inherited a spirit for adventure and taking risks from his parents. In 1767 they had risked everything when they left their home in France to immigrate to the American Colonies.

# Champion Hornpipe Dance Dancer

Leaving home for an unknown place takes a lot of courage. Knowing that you may never return or see your family again is frightening. It is also scary when there is no guarantee you will even arrive safely. But that is exactly what Jacob Durang and his wife Joeann did. They sailed across the stormy Atlantic Ocean in a tiny crowded sea vessel to America. Jacob had just completed twelve years serving in the army of Louis XV, the great-grandson of Louis XIV.

Soon after arriving in the new world, their first child, John, was born in 1768. Four girls and two more boys joined the family in the following years. The Durangs lived close to York, Pennsylvania, where John's father was a barber and hairdresser by trade. This was a good profession because both men and women liked hair styles that needed lengthy preparation several times a week. Many people also wore wigs that had to be curled and powdered.

Speaking three languages, French, German, and English, John's father did well in business. He was soon able to buy a house for his family, a horse and carriage, cows, hogs, and farming utensils. Most people grew their own food. There were no refrigerators, so they pickled vegetables in vinegar and smoked meat to preserve them. Two times a year John and his father took the horse and carriage and traveled one hundred miles to Philadelphia to buy supplies.

Most of the time John kept busy. He attended the German School in York where he studied reading, writing, mathematics, and

BORN: January 6, 1768 in Lancaster, Pennsylvania, the American Colonies
DIED: March 31, 1822 in Philadelphia, Pennsylvania, United States of America

poems. Because paper was scarce, he had to memorize and recite his lessons. He also had a lot of chores to do at home. When he finished his work, he played with friends. They rolled wooden wagon wheels, ran sack races, and played leapfrog and blind man's bluff. They also made kites, and went fishing and swimming in the summer.

But John thought country life was dull. There was never anything exciting to do except at harvest time. Then everybody went into town. There were wagons full of all kinds of things to buy. Singers, dancers, magicians, and puppet shows were everywhere. Everything fascinated John. Able to speak French, German, and English, he asked lots of questions and tried everything he saw and heard.

Dancers especially grabbed John's attention. Many of the dancers he saw at harvest time were dancing masters who traveled from town to town giving dance lessons and performing.

In the 1700s people in the American Colonies thought dancing lessons were part of a good education. Adults believed dancing was good exercise for one's health and physical appearance. It also taught children social manners.

Dancing masters often stayed at private homes for a few days to instruct an entire family. Even George Washington, the military commander and first president, invited dancing masters to visit his home to teach his family because he too liked to dance.

John was seven years old when his father left home to fight in the American Revolutionary War against Great Britain. It was 1775. Wanting to go along, John joined a volunteer group. Boys and men of all ages volunteered even though they were not trained for military service. Many did not have warm clothes or good weapons. When John's group met up with his father's regiment, he was quickly sent home. John was very disappointed.

When independence was declared and John's father returned home, the family moved to Philadelphia. Now eight years old John liked Philadelphia. It was exciting, not dull like the country. During this time there were many celebrations, banquets, balls, and fireworks displays. John appeared in a pageant celebrating the first July 4th in 1776. He was Mercury on a printer's press and Benjamin Franklin's daughter made his costume with a cap and wings. In fact Franklin, who knew John's family well, was working in the same room while John was fitted for his costume.

John's life changed direction when he was twelve years old and he saw a dancer perform a hornpipe dance. Hornpipe dances got their name from the instrument used to accompany the dance. Made from an animal horn or wood, hornpipes are reed instruments with finger holes. John liked the dance a lot because it was so quick and lively. Determined to learn the steps, he asked his father's permission for the dancer to stay at their house and teach him the dance.

Dancing and music were now John's primary interest. He copied and practiced every dance step he saw. He learned to play several instruments. He helped build stage machinery for traveling shows. After three years, he was so skilled that a visiting showman offered him a job to travel with him to Boston, Massachusetts. John was fifteen years old and ambitious. He wanted to know the world, to improve himself, and to travel. So like his parents did years earlier, John set out to an unknown place. But he had uncomfortable feelings. This was the first time he ever did anything without asking his father's permission.

Going from Philadelphia to Boston took several days traveling by ferry boat, stagecoaches, and packet boats used for delivering mail and small packages. John stayed two months in Boston performing and working. He tried to be careful with his earnings, but he did take some dance lessons. When he completed his contract, John headed home. He was extremely nervous. He had had no contact with his family since he left more than two months before. But everyone was happy and relieved to see him and John was glad to be home.

One of the first things John did when he returned was to create a puppet theater in his father's house. With the help of his brothers and sisters, John built a raised stage, constructed two-foot tall wooden puppets, made their costumes, and painted the scenery. He also wrote the stories. Members of his family played all the parts and helped run the theater. It was a complete success and tickets for every performance were sold out.

Throughout, John continued practicing his dancing. So he was ready when he received an invitation to a grand ball. John liked social events when he could dress in fine clothes and display his knowledge of fashion. Usually John did not perform at private parties, but when he was asked to perform his hornpipe dance at the ball he accepted. By chance Lewis Hallam and his theater company from England were performing in Philadelphia at the time. When Hallam heard about John's performance at the ball, he invited seventeen-year-old John to join his company. During the next thirty years John became the first American-born professional dancer. Several times George Washington was in the audience to applaud him.

When the capital of the United States moved from New York to Philadelphia and surrounding cities, John danced in all of the capital cities.

When new theater companies began, John was in the cast of players.

When French ballet dancers came to America to perform, John danced with them.

When the first large circus formed, John traveled with it to perform in Canada, and added clowning, wire dancing, horseback dancing, and making fireworks to his talents.

Self Portrait

Being a professional dancer meant that John earned his living from show ticket sales. Therefore he had to constantly perform and find new audiences. This involved traveling. It also meant creating theaters in empty halls where there were no stages. John was always performing, teaching, or planning new productions. Several times John partnered with other people to create new opportunities for shows. One of these was an amusement park similar to theme parts today.

Entertaining people was important to John. Always listening to his audiences he kept inventing things to amaze them. For example, sometimes for his solo performances he placed a trampoline backstage. Jumping off the trampoline, he could surprise his audience by suddenly landing in the center of the stage. On really special occasions he added fireworks to his entrance.

Family was also very important to John. Throughout his life, his siblings joined him on many of his productions. John married when he was nineteen years old, and had six children of his own. They all performed with him on summer tours through Pennsylvania. After John retired, his children continued performing. His two oldest sons, Charles and Ferdinand, fought in the War of 1812 between the United States and Great Britain. It is believed that they were the first people to sing the *Star Spangled Banner* in public.

When John was born, America was composed of thirteen colonies bounded by British Canada, Spanish Florida, and the Mississippi River. John saw both the new government form and George Washington inaugurated as the first president. In 1822 when John died at age fifty-four, the fourth president, James Madison, was in office. The United States stretched to the Rocky Mountains, and dancing was a popular form of entertainment in America.

# Create A Dance

John Durang was known for his hornpipe dance. A musician even composed music for him titled *Durang's Hornpipe*. He danced his hornpipe dance dressed like a sailor.

**Originally British sailors danced hornpipe dances for exercise when they were at sea. These energetic, quick solo dances fit well in small spaces found on the decks of ships. The sailors held their backs straight and moved their arms and legs as they danced.**

We know a lot about John because he wrote a journal about his life and dancing. As you saw earlier, he also painted a picture of himself dancing his hornpipe dance. His hornpipe dance had "twenty-two movements" or steps. Some were ballet steps and some were popular dance steps of his time. They were all things he liked to do. Many of the stages where John performed were small. They measured twelve by fifteen feet or less. This was very different from the huge halls where Louis XIV performed.

Dances in small spaces do not cover distance. But they can move in all directions:
forward,
backwards,
to one side,
to the other side,
diagonally,
up in the air,
down to the floor,
and around in a circle.
They can also move very fast. To begin your dance, measure an area that is twelve by fifteen feet for your stage.

# Small Space Solo Dance
## Warm Up

- Take four walking steps forward,
- Four walking steps backward,
- Four walking steps to one side,
- Four walking steps to the other side.
- Spin in a circle.

Think of four movements you like to do that you can perform in a small space. They might be movements you learned in dance class. They may be movements you saw others do. Or they may be something you create yourself.

## The Dance

- Begin with a frozen (still) shape or pose.
- Perform your first movement going forward for four counts.
- Do your second movement moving backward for four counts.
- Move your third movement to one side for four counts.
- Let your fourth movement travel to the other side for four counts.
- Spin around in one place.
- End with a frozen (still) shape or pose.
- Repeat your dance moving faster.

How does it feel dancing in a small space? Do you like it?

# Marie Taglioni
## 1804-1884

"This little ugly duckling will never learn to dance." Marie was a young girl when she heard her teacher at the Paris Opera Ballet declare this to her father. Trembling, Marie watched the anger surface to her father's face. After all, he was Filippo Taglioni, the famous ballet dancer. How could she ever carry on the ballet tradition of the Taglioni family?

# Floating in Midair

Marie was pale and quite thin. Her hair was stringy. Her bony arms looked too long hanging down from her rounded shoulders. And yes, she was the third generation of the dancing Taglioni family. Her paternal grandparents were both dancers. Her father, seen in the portrait, two of his three brothers, and both of his sisters were dancers. Her father had even performed at the famous Paris Opera. There he met and married the daughter of a Swedish opera singer. Marie, their first child, was born in 1804 when they were living in Stockholm, Sweden. Her brother, Paul, was born four years later.

While he performed throughout Europe, Marie's father had entrusted his daughter's dance training to a teacher at the Paris Opera. When he learned of her failure at the ballet school, he vowed to turn Marie into the most beautiful dancer the world had ever seen. He would teach her himself!

This was during a time of unrest in Europe. People's lives had been turned upside down by the French Revolution. The ruling of France moved from the King to the people, and a young man named Napoleon became the military and political leader of France. He led France to war with Germany, Italy, Spain, the Austrian Empire, Russia, Egypt, and Syria.

BORN: April 23, 1804 in Stockholm, Sweden
DIED: April 24, 1884 in Marseille, France

When Napoleon was defeated in 1815, the Industrial Revolution was also changing people's lives. Discovering the use of steam for energy, people started using powerful machinery to make products. Skilled craftsmen lost their jobs because factories could produce products faster. People left their farms and moved into cities to work in the factories. These jobs did not pay very well and people were hungry and unhappy in their everyday lives.

This was the world where Marie was growing up. Most cities in Europe still had ballet companies and schools, but changes in government left less money for ballet performances and dancers' salaries. Dancers, like Marie's father, had to keep traveling to different countries to find work. Therefore Marie's family lived in several European cities: Stockholm, Vienna, Milan, and Berlin. Marie learned to speak the language of each place. There was no public education for girls in Europe so Marie's education came from studying ballet with her father several hours every day. Her father demanded perfection and she worked hard to please him because she loved to dance. Paul, her younger brother, also took the classes with her.

In the early 1800s women dressed in long skirts with layers of heavy petticoats underneath. They wore corsets to make their waists look tiny.

For her ballet classes Marie wore a dress with a fitted bodice and knee length layered skirt of muslin cotton. Her thighs were hidden in bloomers. She wore stockings on her legs and light weight slippers on her feet. A black sash was tied around her waist.

In class Marie's father concentrated on her jumping skill. He taught her to jump up in the air, remain still for a moment, and then descend very slowly. Her feet should not make a sound when she landed. Additionally Marie crossed her arms at her wrists, so her arms would not look too long. (Instead of crossing their wrists, ballet dancers usually leave space between their finger tips when their arms form a circle in front of them or over their head.) Marie's father also helped her strengthen her ankles, knees, and back so she could dance *en pointe* (on the tips of her toes). When other dancers stood on their toes, people called it a stunt. But for Marie, rising to her toes and dancing was a way to express herself. She felt like she was floating in midair.

Marie gave her first public dance performance in Vienna when she was eighteen years old. Vienna adored her. Then she danced on the stage at the beautiful huge Paris Opera House. It was important for dancers to succeed at the Paris Opera because Paris was still the world center for ballet. Daily ballet classes continued after her debut, and her father choreographed ballets for Marie to show off her special talents. She became the most talked about ballerina and he the best known choreographer of the time. They both received six-year contracts with the Paris Opera.

In 1832 her father choreographed a ballet called *La Sylphide (The Sylph)* that placed Marie forever in ballet history. The title role was perfect for her because she danced so well *en pointe* and she could look like she was flying in the air. Marie was an instant success. Dance reviewers said, "Taglioni floats like a blush of light before our eyes... in three bounds she crossed the stage from one end to the other, she flew, she never touched the ground... her tireless feet could run over blades of grass without bending them."

*La Sylphide* (*The Sylph*) with music composed by Jean-Madeleine Schneitzhöeffer, is a ballet based on a fairy tale from Scotland. The ballet tells the story of a sylph, a woodland creature, who falls in love with a human man. It is a sad story because the man is going to marry someone else. So his love for the sylph can never be. Marie Taglioni, the first dancer to perform the sylph wore an all white costume. It had a tight bodice and her neck and shoulders were bare. Two small wings were attached to her back. Her bell-shaped skirt made of layers of light weight gauze fell half way between her knees and her ankles. Light weight slippers were tied with ribbons crisscrossing her ankles. Her hair was parted down the middle and pulled back into a bun close to her head.

*La Sylphide* was choreographed at the beginning of a time in the history of arts expression called Romanticism (1830-1870). This time was only a few years after the reign of Napoleon and the beginning of the Industrial Revolution. People were unhappy living in crowded cities and working in factories. They were tired from years of war. So nature settings seemed peaceful and attractive. They sought fantasy and color in their lives. Characters from faraway places fascinated them. Through the arts people found they could celebrate freedom, their feelings, creativity, and beauty.

Therefore *La Sylphide*, a fairy tale of an ill-fated love story set in a nature setting from another place was very popular. As an example of arts expression during the time called Romanticism, *La Sylphide* is called a Romantic ballet. The ballerina's bell shaped skirt is identified as a Romantic tutu.

The ballet made a lot of money for the Paris Opera. Marie and her father were both well paid. They traveled by stagecoach throughout Europe performing *La Sylphide* along with other ballets created for Marie. They never performed in the United States, but for four years they made return trips to St. Petersburg, the capital of Russia. Traveling by boat to England, they appeared several times in London, where Marie danced for Queen Victoria.

Marie even became a popular culture figure. Several products bore her name: caramels, cakes, hairstyles, everyday dress fashions, children's dolls, and even a London stagecoach. Lithographs and drawings exist today of Marie dancing her different roles.

Born into a family of dancers, Marie danced all her life. It seemed natural to her to have a career even though working outside the home was discouraged for women in nineteenth-century Europe. There was plenty of work in the home. Wealthy women supervised servants to do the house work. There were no refrigerators, so fresh food had to be purchased at the market every day. There was no hot running water, so water was fetched from backyard wells or street pumps and heated in large vats over an open fire. Laundry was washed by hand in tubs with scrub brushes, and then pressed by flat irons heated over the fire. Food was cooked on coal fired ranges. Women spent hours arranging dinners, and other events to help their husbands' careers.

The same year she first performed *La Sylphide*, Marie married Count Gilbert de Voisins, a French nobleman. The count expected Marie, as a proper noble lady, to end her career to care for his home and their two children. But Marie loved dancing. She was sure her husband would understand and change his mind so she continued accepting dancing engagements. Unfortunately this meant she was gone for weeks and months at a time.

Traveling from country to country in horse drawn stagecoaches, aboard steamships and ferry boats took time and energy. Riding for hours in a stagecoach over unpaved bumpy roads was uncomfortable. No heat or air conditioning increased the risk of getting sick. Trips were also dangerous because robbers often attacked the travelers. When Marie's carriage was stopped by such a thief, she was able to convince the man to let her dance for him instead of giving up her money. Finally one time when Marie returned home totally exhausted from her tour, the count shut the door in her face. They were divorced.

**Marie Taglioni's performance of the sylph greatly influenced the future of ballet. Her costume, hair style, and the slippers she wore with ribbons crisscrossing her ankles became the image of a ballerina. Her ability to dance *en pointe* and appear to ignore gravity changed the look of ballet dancing. It also changed ballet training. Female dancers learned to dance *en pointe* and male dancers learned to help support the ballerina's balance. Everyone learned to jump higher and stay longer in the air.**

Marie retired from performing in 1847 at age forty-four. She turned to teaching ballet and eventually moved to London, where she taught dancing and manners at court to children of royalty. One of her students was the grandmother of Queen Elizabeth II. In 1884 Marie died at age eighty.

# Create A Dance

Marie Taglioni is known for her jumping skill, appearing to float in the air.

**Dancers begin and end every jump with a *plié* (bending knees). This is one of the rules established by Louis XIV's Royal Academy of Dance.**

# Dancing in Midair
## Warm Up

- Keep your back straight. Bend (*plié*) and straighten your knees slowly.
- Keep your heels on the floor as you bend your knees.
- Try jumping up in the air and landing several times.
- *Plié* before you leave the ground, and after every jump when you land.
- Practice landing so quietly that your feet make no sound touching the floor.

Think of different people and things that leave the ground and go into the air: kites, butterflies, basketball players, bouncing balls. Pick one for your dance.

## The Dance

- Begin with a frozen (still) shape or pose.
- Go into the air at least three times. Be sure to *plié* before and after each jump.
- Move into two different directions.
- Try moving in both a straight path and a curved path.
- Finish with a frozen (still) shape or pose.
- Repeat your dance and see how quietly you can land.
- Pretend you are dancing on the moon and you are weightless.

How high can you jump? How quietly can you land?
Can you look weightless like Marie's father demanded?

# William Henry 'Juba' Lane
## 1825-1852

William Henry Lane was probably the first African American to become a professional dancer. He was born about 1825, three years after the death of John Durang, the first American-born professional dancer. Crowned 'King of All Dancers', William traveled to London and danced for Queen Victoria at Buckingham Palace, just like Marie Taglioni had done three years earlier.

# Lightning Legs, Tapping Feet

Where exactly William was born and who his parents might have been is unknown. However, most of what we do know about his early years occurred in Five Points, New York. New York was a free state, which meant it had abolished the practice of slavery which existed in the United States. William was part of the first generations of people of African heritage in the United States to grow up as free men.

Five Points, New York was close to the docks in lower Manhattan Island (New York City). It got its name because two cross streets plus another street merged together forming five corners or points. At the turn of the nineteenth century the United States, like Europe, entered the Industrial Revolution. Using steam for energy, factories were created to manufacture products. Therefore, as in Europe, many skilled craftsmen and farmers lost their jobs, and people moved to the cities to work in the factories.

Because of its location close to the docks, factories opened in Five Points. It had a large pond to provide fresh water for those businesses. But by 1811 the pond became polluted from overuse and it quickly became an insect-infested swamp. Middle class families moved away.

By the 1820s Five Points was home for poor working people and many immigrants who had arrived at the docks close by. It was also home to newly freed slaves. So people of African, Anglo, Irish, Jewish, and Italian heritages found themselves living together. To people outside, Five Points was an overcrowded slum with disease, unemployment, and crime. But to its residents Five Points was a thriving working class neighborhood.

BORN: 1825 (?) in Five Points, New York (?), United States
DIED: 1852 in London, England

This is where William grew up. He probably did not go to school because public education in the United States was not organized before 1840. Therefore young people in Five Points received their education on the streets and at whatever jobs they found. The streets were where they also learned one another's dances.

The Irish danced jigs and reels. They held their bodies erect and their arms down alongside their bodies as they danced. They moved their legs very quickly tapping the ground rhythmically with their feet. The Africans, identified as Negroes or colored, danced with their whole body. Bending forward at the hips, they performed shuffling and sliding movements with their legs and feet. Their arms and shoulders moved at different rhythms from their legs and feet.

William learned to dance from 'Uncle' Jim Lowe, a jig-and-reel dancer. William became skilled at improvisation. This meant he could quickly imitate other people's dances, and then right on the spot he would create a variation of what he had just seen.

Five Points had a dance hall called Almack's. People went there after work to eat, drink, and have a good time. William made a name for himself at Almack's, where he danced for his supper. He was slim and barely five feet three inches tall, but he commanded attention when he danced. Patrons cheered his variations of the Irish jig steps. They laughed at his imitations of other dancers, and they enjoyed watching William dance. At Almack's William and other dancers blended dance styles and steps and laid the foundation for tap dancing.

William's life changed in 1842 when Charles Dickens, the famous British author, saw him dance at Almack's. Many of Dickens' stories described the hardships of living in slum neighborhoods in England. So when the author visited New York City in 1842, he asked to see Five Points. New York City leaders were shocked because they had planned events at special places. But Dickens insisted on visiting Five Points. There he found Almack's and saw William dance.

Dickens was very impressed. In his book, *American Notes for General Circulation Vol. 1*, he described William's dancing, "... snapping his fingers, rolling his eyes, turning in his knees, presenting the backs of his legs in front, spinning about on his toes and heels... with two left legs, two right legs... all sorts of legs and no legs..."

William was seventeen when Dickens saw him dance. He realized that praise coming from the famous author could help him advance. Five Points had taught William that he had to promote his own future. So he pursued two career changes. First, he assumed a stage name. (Dickens had written his first book in 1836 using the pen name, 'Boz'.) William chose 'Juba' as his stage name.

Juba was the name of a style of African dance that involves rhythm and competition. Dancers form a circle. One or two move to the center. Different dance steps are called out and the dancers in the center perform them. People in the outside circle 'pat Juba', which means stamping feet, clapping and slapping hands, chest, and thighs in time to the dancing. When the center dancers finish a step, everyone performs the 'Juba' step, turning around in a circle lifting and patting one foot on the ground. They chant, "Juba this... Juba that... Juba (add the name of another step)." The dancers perform that movement as the circle of dancers cheers them on with more stamping, clapping, and slapping. Once dancers have shown their moves, they rejoin the outer circle. New dancers enter the center to show their skill.

William's second career change was to seek the title of best dancer. Competitions to prove various skills were a popular form of entertainment. John Diamond, a white man, was considered the greatest Irish jig dancer. So from 1844 to 1845 William competed with John at least three times. Competitions were good publicity for both dancers. Plus they each earned $300 to $500 per competition ($7,000 to $13,000 today).

For their competitions William and John performed six dances. Three groups of judges evaluated them. The first group sat in front of the stage to grade the dancer's style and form. The second group sat to the side of the stage to evaluate the dancer's timing. The third group sat under the stage to listen to the accuracy of the tapping feet on the floor above them.

William lost the first competition with John in Boston. But he won two later challenges in New York, and was recognized as 'King of All Dancers' in 1845. Then he danced with traveling minstrel shows throughout the northeastern United States.

Minstrel shows began about 1830 and were popular until the early twentieth century. They had funny skits, dancing, and music played on banjoes and tambourines. Impersonating the lives of slaves on southern plantations was a central theme of the skits. The performers were white men, who wore burnt cork on their faces to look black.

William is believed to be the first black man to work with a group of white performers in the United States. He even received top billing as 'Master Juba, King of All Dancers'. And in 1848 he crossed the Atlantic Ocean by steamship to join a famous minstrel group in England. Everyone in England had read Dickens' ('Boz's') description of the young black dancer in America and they were anxious to see him dance. Billed as 'Boz's Juba', William, seen in the image, toured with Pell's Ethiopian Serenaders throughout England and Scotland for eighteen months.

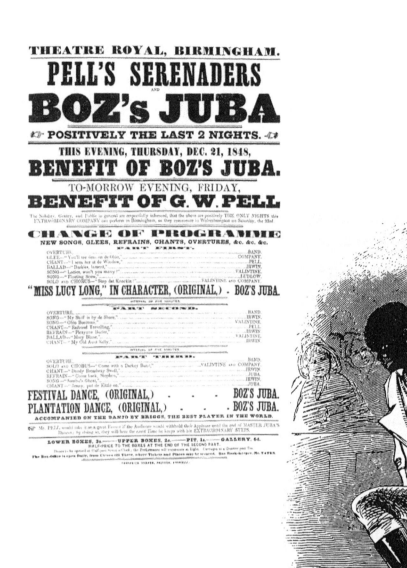

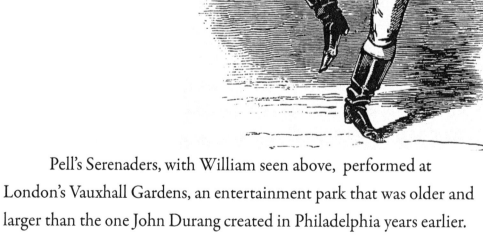

Pell's Serenaders, with William seen above, performed at London's Vauxhall Gardens, an entertainment park that was older and larger than the one John Durang created in Philadelphia years earlier.

Audiences were ecstatic. Critics said his dancing was an original creation. They wrote, "The dancing of Juba exceeds anything ever witnessed in Europe." When the tour ended in 1850, William did not return to the United States. He chose to stay in England. There he performed as a solo dancer in smaller theaters and dance halls until his death in 1852. He was only twenty-seven years old.

Some say William presented authentic pictures of southern plantation dancing by the slaves. Others say he invented tap dancing. Most agree that he created something new and original. He had a profound effect on everyone who saw him dance.

William died nine years before Abraham Lincoln became president of the United States and the American Civil War began. That war also called the War Between the States abolished the practice of owning slaves in the United States.

## Create A Dance

William Henry 'Juba' Lane played with rhythm. People liked watching him dance, but they also listened to the rhythm of his tapping feet. Rhythm is the patterning of accented and unaccented beats. For example the tick-tock of a clock is an accented rhythm. The whirr of an engine is an unaccented rhythm.

# *"Rhythm Story Dance"*
## Warm Up

- Think of a rhythm you hear every day. Practice clapping or stamping it.
- Change the tempo (speed) of your clapping or stamping. Perform slowly and then faster.
- Begin clapping or stamping slowly, gradually speed up, gradually slow down.
- Change the force in your clapping or stamping. Perform it loudly, then softly.
- Begin clapping or stamping loudly, gradually softer. Now try the opposite.

Select one of the following for your rhythm story:

> *Thunderstorm. Slow drizzle accelerates to heavy fast rain, thunder/lightning.*
> *Cuckoo Clock. Ticking hour, minute, and second hands.*
> *Steam Engine Train. Clickety-clack metallic sound of train wheels against the*
> *track traveling very fast, slows down, pulls into station. Stops.*
> *Galloping Horses. Traveling fast. Hear in the distance getting closer. They pass by.*
> *They disappear in the distance.*

## The Dance

- Begin and end in a frozen (still) shape or pose.
- Use the sounds of your hands, feet, and voice.
- Your dance should last one minute. It can stay in one place or move around.

What does listening
to dancing mean?

# Anna Pavlova
## 1881-1931

"One day I shall be the Princess and dance upon the stage of this very theater," Anna proclaimed looking up at her mother. They had just attended a performance of *The Sleeping Beauty* ballet at the Maryinsky Imperial Theater in St. Petersburg, Russia. It was 1889. Anna was celebrating her eighth birthday, and that night changed her life forever.

# Dance Ambassador to the World

Anna was born in the cold month of January, 1881 in St. Petersburg, the capital of Russia. The country has long cold winters with a lot of snow and short cool summers. Russia, the largest country in the world, includes parts of eastern Europe and all of northern Asia. It reaches from the Baltic Sea on the west to the Pacific Ocean on the east, and from the Arctic Ocean in the north to the Black Sea and Caucasus Mountains in the south.

Throughout her life Anna was small in stature, slim, and delicate. She never really knew her father because he died when she was very young. Anna and her mother lived alone in a tiny apartment and her mother worked as a laundress. They did not have much money, but every summer they took a short vacation to the country. They spent afternoons on the porch of their cottage making flower wreathes and telling stories. Anna loved to dance with the birds, flowers, and butterflies.

*The Sleeping Beauty* was one of Anna's favorite stories. So when her mother heard the Imperial Ballet was performing it, she took Anna to see it. After the performance Anna begged her mother to take her to the Imperial Ballet School auditions. But she had to wait two long years until she was ten years old. Finally, when she did go she passed the audition.

Being accepted into the Imperial Ballet School was a great honor. It meant receiving room and board, an academic education, and dance training for six years all paid for by the government.

BORN: January 31, 1881 in St. Petersburg, Russia
DIED: January 23, 1931 in The Hague, Netherlands

Ballet had been popular in Russia for many years. Russian diplomats visiting the court of Louis XIV had seen his court ballets and described them to the czars (emperors) of Russia. The czars then spent great sums of money to create their own ballet productions and ballet school. Like Louis XIV they used many dancers dressed in beautiful costumes. Spectacular scenery filled the stage and a full symphony orchestra accompanied performances. During the nineteenth century choreographers, designers, and dancers including Marie Taglioni and her father came from everywhere to perform there.

Russia became the world center of ballet from about 1885 to 1914. A French choreographer named Marius Petipa, seen in the photograph, headed the Russian Imperial School and Theater for most of that time. He staged over sixty ballets including *The Sleeping Beauty, Swan Lake*, and *The Nutcracker*. Peter Ilich Tchaikovsky, the famous Russian composer, worked with him. Russian ballet was called classical ballet because it used rules and movements set up two hundred years earlier by Louis XIV's ballet masters.

Anna's days at the Imperial School were full. She slept with twenty other girls in one large room. A loud bell woke them every morning, and they quickly dressed in the school uniform, a blue dress. Following prayers and before dance classes they ate bread and butter with tea. After lunch they attended academic classes all afternoon. Classes in fencing, pantomime, acting, music, and different languages filled the evening until bedtime at nine o'clock.

Dance classes were in a large room. There was no furniture except a few benches and a piano for the accompanist. The floor was wood and the ceiling high. Mirrors and large portraits of Russian czars covered the walls. Wooden railings called barres were mounted along the walls. Students placed one hand on the barre for balance as they performed warm up exercises. Besides classical ballet steps, Anna learned dances of other countries. Some days were special because Czar Alexander III and the Empress visited. They had tea with the students and the young dancers performed for them.

The young dancers also studied dance history, and heard of the great Marie Taglioni, who danced in Russia years earlier. Anna idolized Taglioni. She learned that Taglioni was thin and delicate like she was. This was important to Anna because her teachers said she was too small to become a dancer. So when Anna learned that Taglioni was known for her lightness and expressiveness, she decided to concentrate on lightness and expressiveness too.

After six years, Anna graduated in 1899. In exchange for their education, graduates were expected to perform with one of the many ballet companies in Russia.

**Classical ballet companies have ranks. Beginning dancers usually join the corps de ballet. This large group of dancers forms a chorus and background for the ballet. For example, in *Swan Lake*, they are swans on the lake. They dance in unison and form geometric shapes and symmetrical patterns. Some dancers graduate from the corps de ballet and dance in smaller groups. Some advance to solo roles. Finally, a few receive leading roles. Extremely talented female dancers become ballerinas and prima ballerinas.**

Anna never danced in the corps de ballet. Judges gave her solo roles at her graduation. That day she also met her future husband, Victor Dandré, a City Council member and a strong supporter of ballet.

Quickly rising to first soloist, Anna danced the leading role in *Giselle*, a ballet from Taglioni's time. The role of Giselle is very demanding, and Anna's performance was so well received that she soon became a prima ballerina. When Anna danced ballets like *Swan Lake* and *The Sleeping Beauty*, she wore a classical tutu. It had a tightly fitted bodice and a knee length skirt make of sixteen layers of gauze like material. This skirt was shorter than Taglioni's Romantic tutu.

Taglioni had performed in many countries, and Anna dreamed of doing the same. Touring with a small group of Russian dancers, she performed in Paris, Vienna, and London. Everyone loved her dancing, and Anna began spending less and less time in Russia. She

especially liked London, so she and Victor bought a home there named Ivy House. It had a large room for a dance studio and an acre of lawn where they built a lake for flamingos and swans, including Anna's pet swan, Jack. Anna surrounded herself with flowers and cats and dogs.

During these times life in Russia was changing. Many dancers were unhappy with the government's authority over dance companies. Some wanted to choreograph new ballets. Others were creating different ways to dance that did not use classical ballet steps. Additionally throughout the country, people were questioning the czar's power. The poor and working classes were unhappy and angry. Strikes stopped public transportation and cut off food supplies. Riots erupted.

Continued unrest led to the Russian Revolution in 1917 and the czar was overthrown. The Soviet Union was formed in 1922.

Dancers including Anna, who were outside Russia during the revolution, were not able to return home. Some joined Anna to make London a new center for dance. Audiences had cheered performances of Taglioni and the American dancer, William Henry 'Juba' Lane seventy-five years earlier.

With Victor as her business partner, Anna started her own company. She used just a few dancers, very little scenery and often performances were accompanied by a single piano. The company performed excerpts and solos from larger ballets. There was no government funding, but Anna made large sums of money from ticket sales. Barely five feet tall and quite slim, she was always on the go and seemed tireless.

Over the next eighteen years it is estimated that Anna and her company traveled 350,000 miles, visited several thousand cities, and gave over 3500 performances. They performed in Europe, Canada, the United States, Mexico, Costa Rica, Panama, South America, and Cuba. They also danced in Japan, China, India, Burma, Egypt, Java, Singapore, the Philippines, South Africa, Australia, and New Zealand. They performed in huge auditoriums and on very small stages. Often they arrived by train just in time to get to the theater and perform. And many times they had to run back to the station immediately following the performance to catch the train on time.

Taking ballet all over the world, Anna was truly an ambassador for dance. She went out of her way to meet other dancers and learn their ways of dancing. In Germany she visited the dancer

Mary Wigman and the musician Emile Jaques-Dalcroze. In India she met the dancer Uday Shankar, who she invited to join her company. Anna also added Mexican dances and Japanese dances to her company's programs.

Anna had no children of her own, but she adored young people. In 1920 she funded an orphanage for Russian children who lost their parents in the Russian Revolution. After performances Anna greeted young dancers with hugs and encouragement. She introduced her students to dances from different countries and dance styles besides ballet. There are many books about Anna including her own journals. There are also photographs, and a few film clips of her dancing. In 1931 beginning another tour, Anna became ill and died just days before her fiftieth birthday.

## Create A Dance

Everyone who saw Anna Pavlova perform, did not forget her dancing. Many particularly remember her performance of *Le Cygne (The Swan)*.

In 1905 Michel Fokine, seen in photograph, a dancer at the Imperial Ballet choreographed *Le Cygne (The Swan)* for his friend, Anna Pavlova. He used music from *Carnival of the Animals* composed by Charles-Camille Saint-Saëns. The ballerina wore a head piece with feathers alongside the sides of her face. Her costume was a classical white tutu with feathers on the skirt, bodice, and her shoulders. She held her neck long and strong. Her arms quivered like wings. Fokine said, "She danced with her whole body from the crown of her head to the tip of her toe."

# Dancing Candle

(Whole Body Dance)

## Warm Up

- Light a candle and place it so you can watch its flame.
- Blow the flame lightly.

    Watch the flame move in a light breeze.
- Blow harder.

    See how it moves with a stronger wind.
- Watch the candle

    as it burns

    and gets closer to its holder.
- Watch the flame gradually disappear.

## The Dance

- In silence, place your whole body in the frozen (still) shape or pose of a candle.
- Raise your arms up high in front of your face.
- Form your arms and hands into the shape of a flickering flame.

    *A small breeze blows your arms, hands, and fingers.*

    Now a stronger breeze moves them.
- As the candle becomes smaller, your body sinks closer to the ground.
- Finish with a frozen (still) shape or pose as the flame disappears.

## How would you describe dancing a whole body dance?

Anna also choreographed three dances which might be whole body dances. Her dances were titled: *The Dragonfly, California Poppy,* and *Autumn Leaves.*

# Rudolf Laban
## 1879-1958

Rudolf Laban's father was an officer in the military service. Growing up, Rudolf watched many military parades and ceremonies. Fascinated at what he saw, Rudolf became an excellent observer of movement detail. Later he created a way to describe how people move without using words.

# Reading and Writing Dancing

Rudolf was born in 1879 in Pozsony, Hungary where his father was a military governor in the Austro-Hungarian Empire. The empire, the second largest country in Europe, included Austria, Hungary, Bohemia, Moravia, Slovakia, and parts of Poland, Romania, Slovenia, Croatia, and Italy.

Pozsony, surrounded by green hills, sat on the border between Austria and Hungary. It straddled the long Danube River that travels from the Black Forest of Germany to the Black Sea. Today Pozsony is named Bratislava, and it is in the country of Slovakia. Pozsony, as Rudolf knew it, had rich farmlands, vineyards and wineries. It was only thirty-seven miles by steam locomotive from Vienna, the capital of the empire. Slovaks, Hungarians—like Rudolf's family—and Germans lived in Pozsony. Their official language was Hungarian.

The oldest child and only son, Rudolf had two younger sisters. As the son of a military governor, he was always well dressed as his photograph at age three years illustrates. Older boys dressed in shirts, jackets, knee length breeches, long stockings, and ankle high shoes. They also wore sailor style suits and hats.

BORN: December 15, 1879 in Pozsony, Hungary
DIED: July 1, 1958 in Weybridge, England

Rudolf went to school from age six to fifteen and studied Hungarian, Latin, Greek, science, and literature. He also took swimming, horseback riding, fencing, tennis, and rhythmic gymnastics. He was proud of becoming an accomplished horseman, and he especially liked rhythmic gymnastics. Rudolf's mother was an artist, and an uncle was an actor. However, his family did not approve of acting as a career and called his uncle a disgrace. He was not allowed to use the family name when he performed.

Rudolf's parents traveled a lot because of his father's job. Since there were no schools for Rudolf in countries where his father worked, he stayed with his grandparents. They owned a large farm house. Its oval shaped music room with a piano was Rudolf's favorite place. He liked to pick out tunes on the piano and act out stories his grandmother told him. At times he was lonely, but he did enjoy roaming about on his own. He liked sitting in the hills above Pozsony observing the activity.

Puppet shows at the local theaters also inspired Rudolf, and he produced one of his own with two characters: Kasperl and the devil. Kasperl was his uncle, the actor. The devil was named Napoleum after Napoleon, the French dictator.

When Rudolf was twelve years old, he traveled with his father. This was exciting as he got to ride on the railroad, in land coaches, and by boat. He saw the coast of the Adriatic Sea where high cliffs dropped straight down into deep crystal clear blue water. This was very different from the winding Danube River at home. They traveled through the wooded mountains of the Balkan Peninsula that stretched from Central Europe to the Mediterranean Sea before arriving at Istanbul, Turkey, an ancient city on the Bosporus Strait.

One of the largest cities in the world, the eastern part of Istanbul is in Asia and the western part is in Europe. Rudolf met people with different ideas. He heard folk stories, songs, and myths he did not know existed. He saw folk dances, sword dances, and ceremonies he could never have imagined. The religious ceremony of whirling dervishes spinning for ten to fifteen minutes without stopping intrigued him. Traveling the world and seeing military troop formations and parades, Rudolf's father hoped to excite his son about a military life. But for Rudolf these experiences fueled his curiosity about how people express themselves through movement.

Returning home Rudolf, now fifteen years old, became an artist's apprentice and worked with a scene painter at a local theater. The artist taught Rudolf important lessons. First Rudolf learned how to draw and paint. Second he learned to observe people and life very closely. Third he learned to work hard at perfecting his craft and to not expect quick success.

Between 1830 and 1920 *tableaux vivant*—living pictures—was a popular entertainment. Groups of people dressed in costumes and posed to recreate still paintings or other familiar scenes.

Rudolf liked these living pictures, and staged some of his own. Before long he began moving the people from one pose to another, then adding music he created dances.

Life changed again in Rudolf's late teens, when his family moved to Budapest, a much larger city than Pozsony. There was a lot more to see and do as people from different parts of the world visited there. Rudolf liked going to coffee houses and having a good time. Seen in the photograph, he was a handsome young man. About five feet ten inches tall and slim, his hair was dark and he had piercing dark eyes.

In Rudolf's world parents decided careers for their children. To please his father's desire of a military career, Rudolf entered Officers Training Academy in Vienna. Although he only stayed one year, he did direct a dance festival with the cadets at the academy. Finally he had the nerve to tell his father that he wanted a career in art, but he did not mention dance. Reluctantly his father agreed for Rudolf to study architecture at the École des Beaux-Arts in Paris, France.

Early twentieth century saw new forms of artistic expression in Europe, Russia, and the United States, as artists responded to the general unrest of people. Some were upset with their government. Some felt industry and machines were taking over their lives. Many missed sense of community. Some simply wanted more time to relax and enjoy life.

Paris, France had a history as a center for the arts so young artists migrated there. Studying architecture and stage design, Rudolf felt right at home. He arranged shows like ones he created in Pozsony and at the military academy, and he performed at the famous Moulin Rouge cabaret. In addition to his father's allowance, he earned extra money by painting posters and illustrations.

When his father died in 1907, Rudolf felt free to concentrate on dance, and moved to Munich, the arts center of Germany. He performed and taught classes, but he did not teach specific steps like ballet. Rather he used improvisation to create his own movements. He wrote articles about dance, and he also became a leader in a new dance form.

*Ausdruckstanz* was the German name for free dance or dance of expression. This dance did not tell a story as much as it showed ideas or feelings. Movements might look distorted and exaggerated rather than trying to look beautiful. Dancers performed sitting or lying down on the floor as well as in upright standing positions. They usually danced barefoot and wore draped cloth costumes or short tunics. Sometimes male dancers wore trousers and female dancers wore long skirts. They often used masks. Spoken words, percussion instruments like drums and gongs, or even silence accompanied the dancers. Music was not necessary. The stage might be bare with little or no scenery.

Rudolf Laban choreographed and performed *Der Mathematicus* (*The Mathematician*) about 1920. His use of a distorted mask and fingernails in this solo dance suggest that people represented by this character may not be as trustworthy as they seem.

For the next twenty years Rudolf opened twenty-five schools and directed and choreographed for theaters and opera houses throughout Central Europe. Students came from all over to study with him. One student, Mary Wigman, became Germany's leading dancer and started her own company. Rudolf also created movement choirs that were popular in Europe's outdoor festivals.

Members of a movement choir moved as a group to express a common theme. They used everyday movements rather than fancy dance steps. Beginning dancers, both children and adults, participated. Hundreds of people came from different locations to form a movement choir. These choirs were popular because people enjoyed dancing as a group. Audiences liked watching the variations in the group's movements.

The more involved Rudolf became with dance and movement, the more he realized the need to write out movement. This would be useful when assembling movement choirs as dancers could read the movements at home before traveling to the performance. Rudolf studied how others had recorded movement including Feuillet's notation published by Louis XIV. But Rudolf wanted to record all movement, not just ballet steps. Plus he was realizing how much he could learn by observing people move. What body parts are moving?

Where are they moving in space?

Are they moving quickly or slowly?

Are their movements forceful or light?

In 1928 Rudolf published the first version of his system known today as *Labanotation*®. Notation is important for dance like it is for music. It not only records the work of composers and choreographers for all time, but students learn music and dances by reading scores. Like music notation Rudolf's notation uses symbols, as seen in the photograph.

In 1936 the Nazi Party in power in Germany saw Rudolf's notation. Thinking it was a secret code for pulling groups of people together, they placed Rudolf under house arrest. He could not teach, choreograph, or continue his work. Fortunately before World War II broke out, he was able to escape.

Like Marie Taglioni, William Henry 'Juba' Lane, and Anna Pavlova, Rudolf found support in England. Discovering new directions for his work, he developed lessons for teaching dance to children in school. Also analyzing workers' movements in factory assembly lines, he found ways for them to move more efficiently.

Rudolf died in 1958 in England. He was seventy-nine years old. The Laban Centre of Movement and Dance in London and the Dance Notation Bureau in New York City along with university programs around the world continue his work in dance notation and movement analysis. Rudolf wrote several books including his autobiography. Additionally he had seven children. At least four of them followed their father into careers in the arts.

◆◆◆

# Create A Dance

Rudolf Laban liked to observe the effort people use as they move. Based on his observations, he named eight efforts listed below in **bold** for you to try.

## *Effort Dance*

### Warm Up

- **Wring** (water from a dripping beach towel.)
- **Press** (a heavy door closed.)
- **Glide** (smoothly like a talented ice skater.)
- **Float** (in the air like a balloon.)
- **Flick** (a fly from the dinner table.)
- **Slash** (a knife through thick weeds.)
- **Punch** (a punching bag hanging from the ceiling.)
- **Dab** (a drop of water on your nose.)

Some of these actions are strong. Some are light. Which ones do you think are strong and which are light? Which do you think are quick and sudden? Which do you think are slower and not sudden? Select four of Rudolf's efforts that you like to create a dance.

### The Dance

- Begin with a frozen (still) shape or pose of your first selected effort.
- Use one body part to perform your second effort.
- Use another body part to perform your third effort.
- Use your whole body to perform your fourth effort.
- End with a frozen (still) shape or pose of your favorite effort.

## Is dancing with different efforts important? Why?

# Doris Humphrey
## 1895-1958

One of the thousands of young dancers who flocked to see Anna Pavlova dance was Doris Humphrey. It was a Sunday afternoon performance in Chicago, Illinois. For Pavlova it was one of many one-night-stands in the United States. For eighteen-year-old Doris the performance left no doubt in her mind that she must dance on the professional stage.

# Modern Dance Missionary

Doris, an only child, was born in Oak Park, Illinois but grew up in neighboring Chicago. Her father managed the Palace Hotel, and her mother worked as the hotel house keeper. This was not her parents' first choice for professions, but it was a good job and they got their own apartment rent free.

The Palace Hotel sat at the intersection of two busy commercial streets. Clanging trolleys passed by all day and night. The hotel had huge rooms and long tall hallways lit by gas lamps. There was a creaky elevator in a wooden shaft, winding staircases, and lots of open space. The Humphrey apartment, filled with overstuffed furniture, had marble topped radiators.

Doris liked living in the hotel. She was especially fond of all the cats that lived there, and she enjoyed getting to know the hotel's patrons. Many were traveling theatrical families—acrobats, singers, actors, and they taught her how to do cartwheels and other tricks. During the day Doris helped her mother clean the rooms and mend linens. In the evening

BORN: October 17, 1895 in Oak Park, Illinois, United States
DIED: December 29,1958 in New York City, United States

after chores her mother, who had graduated from college as a classical pianist, played the piano for her family. Hoping Doris would become a pianist, she began giving Doris lessons when she was eight years old.

The Humphreys enrolled their daughter in the Francis W. Parker School, a Chicago private school, when it opened in 1901. Doris was a good student in English, history, music, and dance. She did not like math or Latin. She also disliked science because one day the teacher dissected the corpse of a cat. Loving cats, Doris certainly did not want to dissect one.

Being popular at school, she received many party invitations. But her mother hesitated to invite Doris's friends to the hotel. She felt the busy neighborhood and hotel guests might scare them. So Doris spent afternoons playing with her dolls and the cats including White Paws seen in the photograph. But one day her mother hired a bus and took the entire class to see a theater performance. Everyone liked the trip, and Doris felt proud.

Dance classes were special and Doris took two classes a week after school. The teacher, Mary Wood Hinman, had traveled to different countries learning dances. She taught Doris gymnastics, folk, ballroom, clog, and aesthetic dance classes, which included some ballet steps.

When Doris did not show promise with her piano lessons at home, her mother decided that she should concentrate on dancing. They pushed back the furniture in the parlor and Doris danced while her mother played the piano. For all of her thirteen years at Parker School she danced in school productions, assisted her teacher, and choreographed dances for the younger students.

One day Hinman suggested that Doris also study with a Viennese ballet teacher. The new teacher carried a little stick to rap the students' ankles. She also insisted her students eat raw gooseberries before class. The ballet spring concert was Doris's first performance on a real stage outside of school. She was excited. But she was quite discouraged when her feet felt like buckling as she watched the other students dancing *en pointe*. She moaned, "How can I ever be a dancer without feet like that."

During Doris's senior year her mother arranged a performing tour, and Doris got permission to leave school for several weeks. The Sante Fe Railroad sent performers to entertain their workers who were

building the railroad connecting Chicago and Los Angeles. Actors, singers, and another dancer joined Doris and her mother who played the piano. They usually performed in the Railway Men's Clubs' game rooms. Furniture was pushed aside, and the performers changed costumes behind upended pool tables. When the performances occurred in local churches, Doris could not perform because some people objected to dancing in churches. This did not make sense to Doris.

Just after her graduation from Parker School, the Palace Hotel was sold and the Humphreys were fired. Having no place to live, the family moved back to Oak Park to live with friends. The cats had to be given away because the friends did not like cats. But there was no time to be upset because her mother had plans. Doris would teach dance to children and ballroom dance to adults. Her mother would manage the business and accompany the classes.

Doris's father was unable to find another job, hence at age eighteen Doris became the financial support of her family. She was a good teacher, but she really wanted to perform. So the Sunday afternoon when Anna Pavlova, the famous ballerina, was dancing in Chicago, Doris took ten dollars from her earnings and against her mother's wishes went to the concert. (Her mother was upset because the friends they were living with did not approve of dancing on Sundays.)

The concert convinced Doris that she must perform. But for five more years she had to continue teaching dance every afternoon and evening and all day Saturday. Then Doris heard about a new dance school in California, and she enrolled in the 1918 summer course.

Denishawn was a Los Angeles dance company and school founded in 1915 by dancers Ruth St. Denis, seen in the photograph, and Ted Shawn. Students studied old and new dance styles and explored ideas of the Orient, as the Far East was then called. Japanese, Chinese, Siamese, Burmese, Native American, and Spanish dances were all part of the curriculum. Productions were elaborate with beautiful costumes and the company toured and performed extensively.

At Denishawn, Doris was happy. She loved dancing outside on the grass and taking private lessons with St. Denis. She met other enthusiastic young dancers including Martha Graham, who like Doris became a famous dancer. Fortunately Doris also met another student who wanted to teach rather than perform. So when Doris was invited to join the Denishawn Company, her new friend eagerly agreed to teach the dance classes in Oak Park. Doris made sure there would be enough money to support her parents as well.

For ten years Doris danced, taught, and choreographed with Denishawn. She performed all over the United States and spent two years dancing in Asia including Japan, China, Singapore, Malaysia, Burma, India, Java, Ceylon, and Cambodia. Doris became close friends with two other company members: Charles Weidman and Pauline Lawrence. Charles was a dancer and choreographer. Pauline was a musician, who helped with costuming, lighting, and business matters.

There were good reasons to work with Denishawn. There was a steady salary. There were interesting places to travel and perform. There was opportunity to choreograph. But there were also limitations. Members could teach only Denishawn ideas and movements. Tours were long and exhausting, and took time and energy away from creative work. After ten years Doris, Charles, and Pauline discussed changing jobs. Leaving the security at Denishawn was scary, but they wanted to find their own ways to dance. So in 1928 they left and moved to New York City, which was becoming a world center for dance, and they became pioneers in the new dance called modern dance.

This was about the same time Rudolf Laban and others were creating the new dance of expression in Germany. Years earlier Isadora Duncan had also introduced her own style of dance to the world.

These new dance practices had similarities. The movements were not ballet. They had no rules from the past. Dancers were free to create movements to express their own ideas. They danced sitting or lying on the floor as well as standing upright. Barefoot, the dancers wore tunics or close fitting leotards. Women also wore long skirts with slits for leg movements and men wore trousers. They used all kinds of music or no music at all. Sometimes they used scenery and other times they danced on a bare stage against black curtains.

Using their students as dancers, the trio formed the Humphrey-Weidman Group. Pauline accompanied classes and performances and handled all business and technical production affairs. The company performed across the United States often in university gymnasiums, because dance was housed in physical education departments. New York City audiences supported the company, but people outside the city found the dancing unfamiliar and strange. So Doris called their performances her "missionary work".

In 1934 Doris, seen in photograph on previous page, and Charles joined other dancers to establish a summer modern dance program at Bennington College in Vermont. (This program of classes and performances continues today as the American Dance Festival at Duke University.) Additionally in 1932 Doris met and married Charles Francis Woodford, a British seaman, and they had one child, a son.

This was all happening during the Great Depression following the Wall Street Crash of 1929. Many people had no jobs and little money. Doris was still sending money home to her parents so meeting expenses to run a dance studio and company was extremely difficult. To save money Doris, her husband, and son shared a seven room apartment with Charles, Pauline, a young dancer and protégé named José Limón, and always at least one cat.

Never actively involved with politics, Doris was aware of the times. She was twenty-five years old when women earned the right to vote. She taught dance classes for the government sponsored Works Progress Administration (WPA) in the 1930s. She watched her protégé, José, enter military service during World War II. She worried that her own son might be drafted during the Korean War in the early 1950s.

Doris was a dancer, choreographer, teacher, and author. Physically she was five feet three inches tall and slim. Her hair was light auburn in color. One of her dancers wrote that she "was a shaft of light as she sped across the stage". *The New York Times* dance critic, John Martin, compared her dancing ability to being like both "steel and velvet". She choreographed or co-created over one hundred dances, many of which were notated in *Labanotation*® and recorded on film.

When severe arthritis made Doris stop performing at age fifty, she concentrated her energy on choreographing and mentoring young choreographers. As a teacher, she created a new vocabulary for modern dance technique. As an author, she published one of the few books on choreographing, *The Art of Making Dances*. Following her death in 1958 her son, Charles Humphrey Woodford, became a publisher of books about dance.

## Create A Dance

In 1928 Doris Humphrey choreographed a dance titled *Water Study*. The dancers' movements suggested ripples and then waves of water rolling up onto the shore. There was no music. Instead the dancers followed the rhythm and sound of each other's breathing as it was timed with the movement of the breaking waves. Dancers were told to dance from the inside out.

# *Dancing from the Inside Out*
## Warm Up

- Practice taking deep breaths, inhale through your nose, exhale through your mouth.
- Like a balloon, inflate your body as you inhale, and then deflate it as you exhale.
- Inhaling (1) stretch tall to touch the ceiling. Exhaling (2) drop down to the floor.
- Inhaling (3) stretch wide to touch the side walls. Exhaling (4) close into a tiny ball.

Think of four different body parts to lift as you inhale, and lower as you exhale.

## The Dance

- Begin with a frozen (still) small shape or pose.
- Inhaling, lift one body part and then lower it as you exhale.
- Inhaling, lift another body part and then lower it as you exhale.
- Repeat inhaling and lifting two different parts together
    and then lower them as you exhale.
- Finish in a frozen (still) shape or pose.

Think of other variations for your dance. Use different body parts and face different directions.

## How does dancing from the inside out feel?

# Michio Ito
## 1893-1961

Michio Ito was a dreamer. Everyone said he was a little boy who told big stories. And in fact he often said, "Do the impossible!" For centuries and long before Michio was born, Japan isolated itself from the rest of the world. But in 1867, twenty-five years before Michio's birth, a different government gained control. The new rulers wanted to learn about other places. They studied European countries and the United States and adopted some of their ideas.

# East and West Dancing Together

Japan is a cluster of islands separated from the rest of the world by water on all sides. About the size of Germany or California, Japan sits across the Sea of Japan from Korea and on the other side of the Pacific Ocean from the United States. Tokyo, where Michio was born, is a seaport on the Pacific Ocean. Several continental plates meet in Japan, so there are frequent earthquakes, and half of the country is mountainous and covered with forests.

Farming, forestry, and fishing had long been occupations of the Japanese people. But when Michio was born in 1893, Japan had become a manufacturing nation. Factories were making textiles including silk, and industrial plants were producing iron and steel. Having won military victories over China and Russia, Japan was recognized as a world power. Visiting other countries Japanese citizens learned to speak different languages. Michio's own father traveled to the United States to study architecture with Frank Lloyd Wright.

As Michio was growing up, Tokyo was a busy city. Trolley cars, bicycles, and rickshaw carts filled its streets. Michio's parents liked the ideas from Europe and the United States, so Michio and his two sisters and six brothers—one sister was older but Michio was the oldest boy—learned from the East and the West.

BORN: April 13, 1893 in Tokyo, Japan
DIED: November 6, 1961 in Tokyo, Japan

Many children wore kimonos like their parents. It is a T-shaped, ankle length robe that wraps around the body and is held in place with a wide belt. It has a collar and wide full-length sleeves. They wore open heeled sandals with split-toe white tabi stockings on their feet.

But Michio called himself "modern boy". He dressed in western styles of knee length breeches, shirts, knee high stockings, and high button shoes.

Like most children Michio attended school for eleven years. His parents were wealthy so he went to private schools. In elementary school he studied Japanese calligraphy learning to write the symbols with a brush dipped in ink. He also studied flower arrangement. His teachers said that would teach him patience and appreciation of nature and beauty. When he entered middle-high school, Michio had a lot of interests including playing tennis and baseball. He was also creative and imaginative. But too often his mischievousness got him into trouble, and he had to change schools four times.

At age eighteen, Michio enrolled at the Imperial Arts Academy. He tried violin, piano, harmonica, voice, and Japanese dance lessons. He liked music but thought that the Japanese dance was wooden and dull.

Japanese theater and dance is centuries old. One form called Kabuki means Ka (song), bu (dance), ki (technique). It includes the Japanese classical dance called Odori, which began about the same time ballet became popular in the court of Louis XIV's father. Like ballet, Kabuki follows rules and movements passed down for generations. Classical theater and dance tell stories of fights between opposite things like battles between good and evil, and love stories that cannot end happily. Audiences attend classical performances to admire the skill of the dancers performing stories they know.

Kabuki performances include singing and speaking as well as dancing while ballet has no speaking or singing. Also unlike classical ballet, only men perform in Kabuki theater. The movements also look different. Ballet dancers bend their knees to push off the ground into the air with straight legs. Their torsos are straight and their arms move in curved symmetrical pathways. Japanese classical dancers bend their knees to stay closer to the ground as they move with gliding steps. They twist their torsos to form different postures. Their arm gestures are not symmetrical. Moments of stillness emphasize strong emotion.

Japanese performers wear kimonos made of silk and fine materials, and sandals with split-toe white tabi stockings on their feet. White makeup covers their faces. Gestures and postures, not their faces, express their feelings.

Thinking that art should be part of his life, Michio decided to become an opera singer. In 1912 at age nineteen, he set sail from Yokohama to study in Europe. (He learned to speak German before leaving Japan.) As seen in the photograph, he was slim, about five feet eight inches tall, and confident. This was ten years before Anna Pavlova danced in Japan, and thirteen years before Doris Humphrey and Denishawn toured Asia.

European opera disappointed Michio, however he liked dance performances. He saw Pavlova and other dancers perform, but the American dancer Isadora Duncan, who wore Greek tunics and danced barefoot, really inspired him. She had created her own way of dancing. Michio shifted his study to dance and looked up a music teacher he had heard about before leaving Japan.

Emile Jaques-Dalcroze, seen in photograph, a Swiss composer, developed exercises called eurhythmics to teach music using improvisation and movement. Dalcroze students performed barefoot and dressed in tunics like Duncan and the German dance of expression dancers. Students came from around the world to study at the Dalcroze Institute near Dresden, Germany.

When Michio joined the school in 1913, he was the only Asian among three hundred students. Besides music and movement skill, he learned costume, lighting and scene design, stage direction, and choreography. However, World War I broke out between Germany and Japan in 1914, and Michio, a Japanese citizen, had to leave Germany.

He found support in London like Marie Taglioni, William Henry 'Juba' Lane, and Anna Pavlova had earlier (and Rudolf Laban did later). Meeting other artists Michio perfected his English speaking. One writer, William Butler Yeats, was curious about Japanese theater and asked Michio's help with a play he was writing, titled *At the Hawk's Well*. Michio studied hawks at the London Zoo to perform the role of the hawk. Beginning to appreciate his own heritage, he realized that artists of the western and eastern worlds could work together.

But World War I was spreading, so Michio sailed to the United States in 1916. New York City became home for thirteen years. Opening his school in New York, he said, "My teaching embraces the ballet, which trains the legs; acrobatic dancing, which trains the body; Oriental dancing which trains arms; and Dalcroze Eurhythmics which develops the brain to control all three."

Teaching, choreographing and performing kept Michio busy. Some of his dances, seen in this image, reflected growing interest in Japanese dancing, music, and costumes. Additionally Hollywood hired him to act in a silent film. During this busy time Michio married one of his dancers and they had two sons.

In 1929 the Wall Street Crash and the following Great Depression hit the United States. Michio moved his family to Hollywood where he could make more money.

In 1916 Michio Ito choreographed a short solo dance titled *Caprice*. The movements showed the feeling of its music also titled *Caprice*. Later the choreographer changed the music to *Pizzicato* by Léo Delibes for its light plucking sounds. The dance, now titled *Pizzicati*, with its lighting effect and no foot movement remained a favorite of the choreographer.

Michio's move from New York City to Los Angeles was within a year or so of Doris Humphrey's leaving California for New York.

An exciting new industry in the 1930s, motion pictures had added sound and were beginning to add color. Film producers wanted Michio's Asian experience, so he worked on six films during the next ten years. Besides continuing his career as a modern dancer, choreographer, and teacher, Michio also choreographed productions at the Hollywood Bowl, a huge open air amphitheater. He used more than a hundred dancers and live symphony orchestras. Audiences of 18,000 people attended, and Michio became a celebrity. These productions were similar in size and popularity to festivals directed by Rudolf Laban in Europe about the same time. However, Michio focused on movement to interpret the music, and Laban focused on movement to express ideas.

Michio never stopped thinking about East and West working together. But by 1938 World War II was on the horizon. Tension was rising between the United States and Japan. Michio was torn because Japan was his birth place and America had given him a career. He tried to promote understanding between the two nations, but his actions were misunderstood, and the Federal Bureau of Investigation (FBI) began watching him. When Japan bombed the United States Naval Base at Pearl Harbor near Honolulu, Hawaii in 1941, Michio was detained. He was sent to an internment camp in Montana, and his family returned to New York. Charges were never filed, but Michio was deported to Japan in 1943.

Returning to a firebombed Tokyo was devastating. But fortunately at the end of the war, he was able to teach and choreograph again. When the 1964 Tokyo Olympics invited him to stage the opening and closing ceremonies, Michio planned to show the East and West working together. Unfortunately he died in 1961 before he could see his dream materialize. He was sixty-eight years old.

When Michio first arrived in the United States in 1916, he had said, "In my dancing it is my desire to bring together the East and the West. My dancing is not Japanese. It is not anything—only myself." He used his eastern and western roots to create his way of dancing and to choreograph over one hundred dances. Books have been written about him, countless people studied with him, and dance companies continue to produce his work.

## Create A Dance

Michio Ito called some of his dances dance poems. He felt single gestures (movements) or body postures (shapes) express an idea or feeling clearly like poetry. Like many poems, some of his dances—*Pizzicati* for example—were short, lasting only a minute or so.

Consider the haiku poem below. Haiku, an ancient form of Japanese poetry, has three lines and seventeen syllables divided into five, seven, and five syllables per line. It usually describes opposite images, often from nature.

> *Leaves silently swirl.*
> *Wind rips through the countryside.*
> *Birds scatter above.*

As part of teaching technique, Michio created two sets of arm movements. One was strong, angular, abrupt. The other was soft, curved, fluid.

# *Poetry Dances*
## Warm Up

- Moving both arms together, practice soft, curved, fluid movements.
- Moving both arms together, practice strong, angular, abrupt movements.
- With one arm perform strong, angular, abrupt movements.
- With the other arm perform soft, curved, fluid movements.

Reading the haiku poem on the previous page:

- Move one arm to express the feeling described in the first line.
- Move the other arm to express the feeling described in the next line.
- Move both arms together to express the feeling described in the third line.

- Create a shape with your whole body to express the first line.
- Create a shape with your whole body to express the second line.
- Create a shape with your whole body to express the third line.
- Select one moment in your dance poem to be perfectly still.

## The Dance

Recite the poem as you dance. Remember to include a still moment.

- Create a frozen (still) shape or pose for the beginning of your dance.
- Form the first body shape and perform the arm movement for the first line.
- Form the second body shape and perform the arm movement for the second line.
- Form the third body shape and perform the arm movement for the third line.
- Create a frozen (still) shape or pose for the ending of your dance.

## Do you like dancing poetry? Why?

# Mrinalini Sarabhai
## 1918 - 2016

"I am a dancer," declared five-year-old Mrinalini. She and her father were sitting together on the veranda as they did every evening. Sharing a special bond, her father chuckled at his youngest child's determination. Born in 1918, Mrinalini had two older brothers and one older sister. They lived in Chennai, a large city, on the southeast coast of India.

# Turning Old into New

The Republic of India is the seventh largest country in the world. Its coastlines face the Arabian Sea, the Indian Ocean, and the Bay of Bengal. India shares land borders with Pakistan, China, the Republic of Nepal, the Republic of Bangladesh, and the Union of Myanmar. India is also home to the Himalayas, the highest mountain range on the planet.

Centuries old, India was an early center of trade routes connecting the eastern and western parts of the world. Due to its important location the United Kingdom colonized the country in the nineteenth century. However, in 1947 India gained its independence. Today India remains a society of many ethnicities. Its official language is Hindi, and English is a secondary language for government and business.

India is proud of its history and culture. For example women continue to wear saris, which first appeared about 600 BC. A sari is a long piece of fabric that wraps around the waist and drapes over one shoulder. A long skirt and a short sleeved blouse, cut off above the waist, are worn beneath the sari. Men wear trousers under knee-length tunics. Everyone wears sandals outdoors. Inside their homes they walk barefoot, leaving their shoes at the door.

Mrinalini's parents liked ideas from the western part of the world. Her father had been educated in England and the United States, and her brothers, like all boys in wealthy families,

BORN: May 11, 1918 in Chennai, India
DIED: January 21, 2016 in Ahmedabad, India

left home at age seven to attend boarding school in England. As a result, Mrinalini hardly knew her brothers as she was growing up. Her father, a successful barrister, seemed to know everyone, including Mohandas Karamchand Gandhi, the leader of the Indian independence movement against the United Kingdom. Teaching non-violent civil disobedience, Gandhi inspired Dr. Martin Luther King, Jr. and other civil rights leaders.

Although Mrinalini adored her father, she and her mother did not get along well. Mrinalini, seen in photograph, was thin and her hair was short. Her mother said she was too skinny and not beautiful like her sister. When Mrinalini would not eat, her mother rapped her knuckles. When she was mischievous, her mother scolded her and locked her in the bathroom.

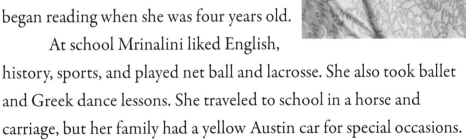

However, Mrinalini was fond of her ayah. Ayahs were women who cared for the children of wealthy families and the British settlers. With her ayah's help Mrinalini learned to speak English, and began reading when she was four years old.

At school Mrinalini liked English, history, sports, and played net ball and lacrosse. She also took ballet and Greek dance lessons. She traveled to school in a horse and carriage, but her family had a yellow Austin car for special occasions.

Unexpectedly and suddenly one day Mrinalini's father died. Twelve years old, her life became very sad. She cried for days alone

and spent hours reading in the large mango trees in her yard, devouring the books of Jane Austen and other authors. After her husband's death, Mrinalini's mother became actively involved with women's rights and Gandhi's fight for independence. Helping others less fortunate, she became a role model for her daughters, and the sisters grew very close.

Mrinalini was fifteen years old when she left home—for the very first time—to attend school in Switzerland. Traveling by ship and train she saw Cairo and Port Said, the Isle of Crete, Naples, Pompeii, Rome, Venice, Paris, and London. One day while visiting Austria and Germany she heard Adolf Hitler speaking at a rally. She did not like the sound of his voice.

The only Indian student at school, Mrinalini was unhappy and home sick. But her knowledge of British and European authors pleased her teachers, and they asked her to write in the school magazine. She began liking Switzerland. The air was clear and cold, different from the hot humid days at home. Mountains and snow completely contrasted the flat coastal plains of Chennai. She enjoyed the changing seasons, and declared her love of nature and vowed to protect it.

Returning home after two years, her mother wanted her to attend Oxford University in London, but Mrinalini had other ideas. She wanted to dance. No one in her family had ever done it, but she was determined. And she found a school in Chennai.

India's classical dance is over 2000 years old. It dates back to a scholar named Bharata. His writing, *Natya Shastra*, identified parts of a dance performance. These included body movements; poetry, song, reciting, music, and rhythm; costumes, makeup and jewelry; and expression of moods and feelings. Bharata wrote centuries before Louis XIV's ballet masters in France and also before early dance teachers in Japan recorded their movements.

Bharata Natyam, also spelled Bharatanatyam, is one of several classical Indian dance styles. It was first performed as a solo dance by female temple dancers during religious services because dancing had a close relationship with religion. However, when India was colonized by outside countries, dancing lost its place in society. But during the twentieth century, ladies of the upper classes began performing Bharata Natyam because it told stories from ancient literature and their culture.

One of those ladies was Rukmini Devi Arundale, seen in the photograph. She had wanted to study ballet when she saw Anna Pavlova dance. But the ballerina encouraged Arundale to study her own classical dance instead, so she opened the school in Chennai where Mrinalini received private lessons with her first dance-guru.

Historically, Bharata Natyam performances occur in small spaces and last about two hours. First the dancer bows to her teacher and the audience. Then musicians strike cymbals and begin to sing. They play different instruments throughout the performance. Combining reciting, singing, and dancing, it is similar to Kabuki theater. Like other classical dance forms, parts of Indian classical dancing tell a familiar story while other parts show the dancer's skill. Like classical ballet dancers, Indian classical dancers hold their backs erect. However, Indian dancers perform with a deep knee bend. Dancing barefoot, they stamp the ground rhythmically.

Indian dancers wear variations of the sari. This is like Kabuki performers who wear the traditional kimono. Images of birds, flowers, and leaves are woven into the colorful fabrics of the sari. Bands of fifty or more bells wrap around each ankle. Rings, gold bands, and bracelets adorn the dancer's neck, arms and hands. Her eyes are penciled and elongated. Jewels, flowers, and tassels are in her hair, which is pulled back in a bun or long braid. This is different from the white makeup covering the faces of Japanese Kabuki performers.

To become accomplished in Bharata Natyam, Mrinalini, seen above, had to learn how to tell a story using the movement of her body. She had to master rhythmic timing with her feet and body movement. Holding her body erect, her feet had to move with her hand and eye movements. Sometimes the lower and upper parts of her body moved together. Other times they had to move in opposite directions. Throughout she had to bend her knees and keep her heels close to the ground.

After training in Chennai, Mrinalini went to Bengal in northeastern India to study with Rabindranuth Tagore, the famous poet, artist, and social reformer, seen in the photograph.

When Mrinalini arrived in 1938, Tagore was seventy-seven years old. He encouraged her to experiment with classical dance, and find her own way to dance and choreograph. She studied many Indian dance forms, and her cultural heritage.

Following her work with Tagore, Mrinalini presented dance concerts in New York City. However, her travels convinced her that she wanted to return home to India to dance. In 1942 she married Vikram Sarabhai, an Indian physicist, and moved to his home in Ahmedabad on the western side of India close to the southern border of Pakistan. The Sarabhai family was wealthy and well-known in industry. Not only did they expect Mrinalini to continue dancing, but they also supported her interest in helping others less fortunate.

At that time the fight for India's independence from the United Kingdom was gaining support. One day at a procession protesting British rule, a shell from a policeman's gun blew up in Mrinalini's face. Seriously hurt, she had a long slow recovery, and her sight was permanently impaired. But this did not change her desire to dance. During her recovery she traveled to England with her husband and presented concerts and lectures about Indian dance.

Returning to Ahmedabad, independence had been won and they opened Darpana Academy of Performing Arts to teach dance, drama, music, puppetry, and Indian cultural studies. They also had two children, a son and a daughter. Mrinalini was able to continue dancing because her husband cared for the children when she performed. With her own company, she danced in London, Paris, Egypt, South America, and Mexico.

Mrinalini created over fifty dance dramas. Her performances began with classical dances. Then still using classical movements, she experimented. Instead of a single female dancer performing, there might be a group of both male and female dancers. Instead of dancing in a small space, the dancers spread over a larger area. Besides dancing stories from ancient literature, she danced about the environment, women's rights, and other issues. Often she introduced her performances by explaining to the audience why she thought the subject of the dance was important.

Additionally Mrinalini began writing again. She wrote books for children using Indian art works. She published articles about classical dance. She wrote her autobiography and created plays about social issues.

People credit Mrinalini with introducing Bharata Natyam to the world, like Anna Pavlova did with classical ballet. The Darpana Academy of Performing Arts she established in 1949 continues today with students attending from around the world. For Mrinalini dancing is about living. She believed that dancing mirrors life: it expresses both its beauty and its ugliness.

## Create A Dance

Bharata Natyam has many movements to master; some are very small. These include movements for the head, eyes (eyelids, eyeballs, and eyebrows), nose, cheeks, lower lip, chin, neck, hands, stomach, chest, waist, legs (thigh and calf), and feet.

# *Dancing Eyes*

## Warm up

- Looking in a mirror, try dancing with your eyes. Use your eyelids, eyeballs, and eyebrows.
- Without moving your head look up, down, to one side, to the other side.
- How many ways can you move your eyes without moving your head?

**Bharata Natyam dancers express the following feelings in their dancing: love, valor, pity, wonder, laughter, fear, disgust, anger, tranquility.**

Read the following story and express the words in **bold** with your eyes.

*KC's Birthday*

*KC looks around in* **wonder**.

*Gifts are everywhere.*

*One package smells funny. KC looks* **disgusted**.

*KC is* **angry** *and does not open it.*

*Another package slips from KC's hands. It sounds like something breaks.*

**Afraid**, *KC unwraps the package. It is broken. KC is* **sad**.

*KC opens another package. It is perfect. KC* **laughs** *and feels* **calm** *again.*

## The Dance

- Bow to your teacher and your audience to begin your dance.
- Your classmates can accompany you with bells, cymbals, and other percussion instruments.
- Dance the story using your whole body, but dance the words in bold with your eyes.
- Create a frozen (still) shape or pose to end your dance.

## Is dancing with your eyes easy? Why do you think?

# Pearl Primus
## 1919-1994

As a little girl, Pearl Eileene Primus listened in awe to her father and uncles telling stories about their adventures in Africa. Deep down inside her own quiet space, Pearl vowed that she too would visit that great continent—that magic place—the home of her ancestors. Pearl was born in 1919 in a poor neighborhood of Port of Spain, Trinidad, the southernmost island in the Caribbean Sea. When she was two years old her family, seeking a better life, migrated to the United States.

# "Earth Dancer"

Pearl, her parents and her two younger brothers lived in a community of West Indian immigrants in New York City. Although the practice of slavery had been abolished in the United States in 1865, the country remained racially segregated. People with dark skin, like Pearl, were still called Negro or colored. They lived in separate neighborhoods, attended separate schools, and even had separate restrooms in public places.

It was not until 1954, when Pearl was an adult, that times began to change. The United States Supreme Court ended school segregation, and that ruling fueled the civil rights movement led by Dr. Martin Luther King, Jr. during the 1950s and 1960s. Inspired by Mohandas Karamchand Gandhi in India, the movement raised expectations for black people in the United States. They eventually became identified as African Americans.

Pearl's father was the superintendent of an apartment building, and he earned extra money shoveling coal. Her mother took in laundry. Closely supervised by their parents, Pearl and her friends rarely went out on their own. However, when they were alone, and they were bullied, they fought back.

Pearl did not see the color of her skin as a reason to be considered different. Rather she was ambitious and seized opportunities.

BORN: November 29, 1919 in Port of Spain, Trinidad
DIED: October 29, 1994 in New Rochelle, New York

She was also cheerful and funny, as seen in the photograph, but sometimes she did get angry. Other times she simply lost herself in thought.

Understanding the importance of education, Pearl was a good student. Imaginative and creative she loved to write poetry. To one teacher's dismay she doodled sketches of nature images on her papers with turquoise-colored ink, her favorite color. Strong jumping legs and a sturdy body made her a good athlete. She also took dance lessons offered free by the government's Works Progress Administration (WPA).

Earning acceptance into Hunter College High School and then Hunter College, she hoped to become a doctor. But when her skin color denied her a lab technician's job, she changed course. Having difficulty finding a job, she auditioned for and won a scholarship to a New York City dance group.

**New Dance Group formed in 1932 during the Great Depression. Times were hard and people were unhappy. With 'dance is a weapon' as its motto New Dance Group used dance performances to bring attention to social injustices. This was the reverse of Louis XIV, who used dance to show beauty and order.**

Joining New Dance Group in 1941 opened a huge door for Pearl. Members were expected to dance about things important to them, so Pearl passionately researched African dances—pouring over books, pictures, everything she could find. Her first dance was titled *African Ceremonial*.

At the same time she was studying modern dance with Doris Humphrey, Charles Weidman, and Martha Graham. She also danced with Belle Rosette, a West Indian dancer from her native Trinidad, and performed in Broadway theaters, night clubs, and at freedom rallies and political gatherings. She

became good friends with both the African drummer and dancer Asadata Dafora from Sierra Leone, seen in photograph, and the black American poet Langston Hughes.

Many of Pearl's solo dances, called 'message dances', told audiences about the experiences of Africans and black Americans. One of her dances, *Strange Fruit*, showed a white woman's reaction to a lynching; *Hard Times Blues* protested the lives of sharecroppers; and *The Negro Speaks of Rivers*, shown in the photograph on the next page, was based on Hughes's poem by the same name. Subjects of Pearl's dances plus her participation in human rights rallies drew the attention of the Federal Bureau of Investigation (FBI). She was never charged with anything, but FBI surveillance followed her throughout her life.

At Pearl's debut concert in 1943, critics noticed this short, muscular, dark skinned woman. When John Martin, the dance critic of *The New York Times*, described Pearl as "a remarkably gifted artist... entitled to a company of her own and the freedom to do what she chooses with it," Pearl became even more determined to dance. (Prior to this, black dancers seeking careers in modern dance were discouraged. Katherine Dunham had experienced success, but she was a rare exception.) However, Pearl did not stop her university studies in anthropology and education.

Visiting the southern United States in 1944, Pearl experienced lives of sharecroppers picking cotton. She was "bewildered and numb" by the "poverty" and "intensity of the hatred and fear" she witnessed with "both black and white" people. As a result, she organized her first company to dance these stories. Three dancers, a drummer/percussionist, a narrator/singer, and a pianist stuffed themselves into a station wagon, dragging a small trailer.

Touring the United States in the 1940s was not easy for people of color. Many restaurants, hotels, and gas stations refused them service, but black colleges treated the company like royalty. They performed African dances Pearl was researching, message dances, and spirituals. Dancing barefoot and bare legged, Pearl wore dresses with full skirts. The African dances used traditional costumes.

In 1948 Pearl's lifelong dream came true. The Julius Rosenwald Foundation awarded her a grant to visit Africa and research dance. The foundation, inspired by the work of Booker T. Washington, provided educational opportunities for persons of African heritage. Pearl would finally see Africa and dance with people who dance as part of their daily lives.

The second largest continent in the world, Africa is surrounded by bodies of water, except for the Isthmus of Suez connecting it with Asia. It has both the world's largest desert, the Sahara, and its longest river, the Nile. Grasslands, dense rainforests, tropical plants, unusual animals, birds, and insects exist there.

**Dancing and music have always been part of African culture. Beliefs and stories are kept alive through drumming, dancing, and singing. Dancers dance bare foot, the flat surface of their feet pressing the earth. Unlike classical ballet dancers who push away from the ground, African dancers embrace it.**

African dance is also polyrhythmic. The hands might clap one rhythm, as the feet stomp another one, and the hips or shoulders may move in a completely different one. Except when jumping, the dancing body bends forward and hips and knees are usually bent. Movements may be explosive jumps or pounces. Or they may flow and ripple through the torso, legs, and arms. Sudden fast spinning also occurs.

Movements are passed from generation to generation during ceremonial celebrations. When dancers master moves, they improvise new ones. They mimic animals and living things, daily life, and human experiences. African dancers think more about 'how they feel' rather than 'how they look' when they are dancing. Drums, flutes, horns, xylophones, stringed instruments, bells, rattles, and other percussion instruments accompany dancing.

African dance has existed in American culture since slaves first arrived from Western Africa in the seventeenth century. The nineteenth-century minstrel shows created imitations of African dance and song. Early twentieth-century social dances like the Charleston copied African dance movements. And in 1934 Dafora fascinated New York City theatergoers with his production of African ceremonial dances. But it was decades before African-American dancers were recognized as serious performers.

Leaving New York City's crowded noisy concrete streets for West Africa's rich green countryside was quite a change for Pearl. She was unbelievably happy at times, but also very lonely at others.

Meeting people from thirty different culture groups, Pearl kept detailed journals, describing all that she saw. She took photographs and filmed dances as she eagerly tried everything. It was important to her to keep the dances authentic, exactly the way African dancers performed them.

Returning home eighteen months later, Pearl was a different person. She began wearing African style clothing all the time. This meant ankle length wrap skirts, blouses, pull-over robes, and head scarves. Gold and silver bracelets dangled from her arms, jewelry adorned her neck and ears.

Anxious to learn more, Pearl visited Trinidad, her birthplace. Caribbean dances have African roots because until the mid-1800s West Africans, many on their way to the United States, were brought to the Caribbean Islands as slaves.

In Trinidad Pearl met Percival Borde, a talented drummer who joined her company. The following year they married and opened the Primus-Borde School of Primal Dance in New York City. Thus began a twenty-five year relationship teaching and performing together. They had one child, a son, Onwin Babajide Primus Borde, who became an accomplished drummer like his father.

Pearl died in 1994 at age seventy-four. Throughout her life she knew the pain of rejection based on the color of her skin, but refused to let it stop her. About five feet two inches tall and always self-confident, she looked "regal" and "majestic". Her dancing was powerful and strong. Her "soaring high leaps" left audiences gasping. Martha Graham said Pearl had the "strength of a panther".

Known as a story teller, Pearl was always teaching in studios, universities, and on African soil. Visiting schools, she introduced many children to African dance. An inspiration to younger dancers, her efforts placed African dance in education curriculum.

Her choreographic output was prolific. Her work differed from the minstrel shows in William Henry 'Juba' Lane's time that mocked the plantation slaves. It also contrasted dances of some of her peers in the 1960s and 1970s that showed bitterness and anger. Rather, not unlike Mrinalini Sarabhai in India, Pearl's dances reached out to inform audiences about issues important to her.

Besides several honorary degrees, Pearl earned a Ph.D. in educational psychology and anthropology at New York University in 1977. As a dance ambassador, Pearl initiated projects with governments in the West Indies and nations of Africa. Her mission was always to educate about African dance and culture and to help African-American dancers feel proud of their heritage.

Today boxes containing over 20,000 items from Pearl's life are in the American Dance Festival Archives at Duke University.

# Create A Dance

Pearl Primus identified African dance movements as "the walk and all its variations... the leap, the hop, the skip, the jump, falls of all descriptions, and turns which balance the dancer at the most precarious angles to the ground".

## *Earth Dancing*
### Warm Up

- Barefoot, try the different movements Pearl listed.

The earth is important to African dancers. This is where roots live, and life begins. Dancers keep contact by thumping and tapping it like drummers make contact striking their drums. Pearl called this "hugging the earth".

- Try "hugging the earth" as you thump and tap the ground with your bare feet.

African dancers observe nature. They mimic movements of animals and other living things. They dance stories about things they have seen and are true to them.

- Select an animal or insect for your dance story.
- Create movements for your animal or insect dance story.

### The Dance

- Form a circle with your friends.
- Take turns performing your animal and insect dances.
- Perform so it is true and meaningful to you.
- Begin and end with a frozen (still) shape or pose "hugging the earth".

## Why do you think Pearl called herself "Earth Dancer"?

# Amalia Hernández
## 1917-2000

"Yes, Amalita," as her father called her, "you may learn to dance, if you do it only at home, never show your legs, and dance only for me and your uncles." Amalia was happy with her father's answer. She knew if she studied hard and patiently waited that one day she would get to dance like she wanted. Amalia was born in 1917 in Mexico City, the capital of Mexico.

# Celebrating History

Mexico sits between the United States on its northern border and Belize and Guatemala on its southern border. The Pacific Ocean touches its western shore and the Gulf of Mexico washes its eastern shore. Mexico City, the largest city in Mexico, rests in a wide valley of high plateaus at the center of the country.

Long before Amalia's birth, Mexico's boundaries extended into what is the United States today. For centuries before Christopher

Columbus visited America in 1492, different groups of native people lived throughout the Americas. Among these were the Aztecs, seen in the illustration, in the illustration, who settled in central Mexico. They built pyramid-temples, used mathematics, astronomy, medicine, theology, and created their own calendar. But everything changed when Hernán Cortés, the Spanish explorer, arrived in 1521 and claimed Mexico for Spain.

It took three hundred years for Mexico to win its independence from Spain. As a result, many Mexican citizens are mestizos—part Spanish and part native Mexican. Spanish became Mexico's primary

BORN: September 1, 1917 in Mexico City, Mexico
DIED: November 5, 2000 in Mexico City, Mexico

language. Separation from Spain in 1821 marked the beginning of years of unrest and fighting for Mexico. The Mexican-American war broke out when the United States annexed Texas in 1845, and Mexico lost some of its northern territory to the United States. And then France invaded Mexico, and the country was again ruled by outsiders. However, in 1862, Mexican fighters unexpectedly defeated the French, and Mexico was independent again.

But in 1910 the Mexican people revolted against their own government. Their president had become a dictator. Foreign companies and large land owners were buying Mexico's sugar, rum, and rice plantations. So citizens were working like slaves on land that they could never own. When fighting broke out, everyone including women, seen in the photograph, participated.

Amalia was born as the Mexican Revolution was ending in 1917. Amalia's father was a wealthy businessman and politician. The family which included Amalia, her parents, two brothers, and two sisters lived in a big house in Mexico City.

They spent summers at their ranch in Tamaulipas in the northern desert. Amalia liked the ranch because she learned songs and dances of the workers. She was proud of her mestizo heritage.

In Mexico City the weather is hot and dry from February to June, rainy and humid until November, and then cooler and dry into February. Amalia's brothers wore white cotton shirts and pants and leather sandals. Large sombreros—wide-brimmed hats—protected them from the sun and rain. Amalia and her sisters wore white cotton blouses and skirts embroidered with bright colors and sandals.

Wealthy women like Amalia's mother stayed at home to care for their families and run the household. Children attended school from age six until they were fourteen years old. So after one year in kindergarten, they spent six years in elementry school and three years in secondary school. Then they decided if they wanted to go on to upper secondary school and prepare for college.

Amalia was always creating dances, but dancing on stage was not proper for young ladies. When her father did give her permission to take dance lessons, he kept her under his watchful eyes. He built a studio close to the house, and hired private tutors. There were two classical ballet teachers. One had danced with Anna Pavlova and the other was a soloist at the Paris Opera. Amalia also studied Spanish dancing with La Argentinita, seen in the photograph, a famous dancer born in Buenos Aires, Argentina and trained in Spain.

Spanish dance includes several different styles. Performers hold their backs erect like classical ballet dancers. Their arms may move symmetrically over their heads and out to the side like ballet dancers. But they may also move their arms in snake like movements and quick flicks of the wrist. Similar to classical Indian dancers, Spanish dancers stamp and tap rhythms with their feet. However, instead of dancing barefoot with ankle bells, they wear shoes or boots with one-to-three-inch high heels. Some play castanets on their fingers or strike tambourines with their hands to accent the rhythm. Female dancers wear long, often ruffled, skirts with tight fitting bodices. Sometimes they wear shawls over their shoulders. Male dancers wear trousers with short fitted jackets. Spanish dancers look proud and hold their bodies tall.

When Amalia was fifteen, La Argentinita invited her to perform with her, but Amalia's father refused. Wealthy girls did not work, and they certainly did not dance outside of home. When Amalia went ahead and did it, her father cut off her allowance and stopped her lessons.

This gave Amalia the chance to try different dancing. For years she had watched the workers dancing at her father's ranch so she joined an agricultural center where folk dance lessons were free. Disguised in baggy clothes and dark glasses, Amalia danced at the center for several months, until one day her father followed her. He dragged her home in his Cadillac car, but Amalia had already decided to dance folk stories.

At seventeen she married a young lawyer, and soon had her first child, a daughter. But her husband—like her father—did not want her dancing, and they quickly divorced. Over the next twenty years Amalia married three more times. She had another daughter and a son. None of the husbands appreciated her love of dance, so each marriage ended in divorce as she continued dancing.

When Michio Ito brought his company to Mexico to perform, one of his dancers, Waldeen, seen in photograph, decided to settle there. Amalia studied and performed with Waldeen for several years as Waldeen became a modern dance leader in Mexico.

In 1934 the government had built a beautiful cultural center, the Palacio de Bellas Artes, in Mexico City. Parts of the building were marble and decorated with crystal and glass. Murals and sculpture depicting Mexico's history covered the inside walls. Both Waldeen and Amalia taught there, but the management did not want Amalia's folk dancing. So in 1952 Amalia left the Palacio with eight students and started her own company, Ballet Folklórico de México. To do this she sold the house she owned and her share of family jewels. She also pawned her father's Cadillac.

About this time black and white television service arrived in Mexico, and Amalia's dancers entered a televised talent competition. Winning the contest, the company performed on television for sixty-seven weeks straight. This meant Amalia had to choreograph a new dance every week. The company became so popular that the Bureau of Tourism hired it to publicize Mexico. Finally even Amalia's father accepted her dancing.

1959 was a big year for the company. It represented Mexico in the Pan-American Games in Chicago. Ordering government support for the company, Mexico's president challenged Amalia to create the finest dance company in the world. Winning first prize in the International Theatre des Nations Festival in Paris, France in 1961, Ballet Folklórico de México became internationally recognized.

Dancing had always been part of Mexico's history, and Amalia researched that history. She studied architecture, sculpture, and art. She read legends and stories. She visited towns and festivals all over the country to learn whatever dances she found. These were not dances with centuries-old recorded rules and steps performed for audiences. Rather like Pearl Primus in Africa, Amalia filmed people dancing together in the fields and town squares.

Showing the spirit of Mexico became Amalia's focus. She used ideas from the dances she saw, and added steps from her own dance training. She bought clothes at local markets and remade them with brightly colored fabrics. She added layers of skirts and placed fancy trim everywhere. Headpieces grew to several feet tall with feathers and ornaments decorating them.

Ballet Folklórico de México performances are pictures of Mexico and its history. Some dances tell stories of the native cultures like the Aztecs founding their capital city before Cortés and Columbus arrived. Some recall life during the Spanish and French conquests and also during the Mexican Revolution when women fought alongside men. Others are regional dances discovered by Amalia showing present day celebrations. Musicians perform with the dancers. There are marimbas; mariachi bands with violins, trumpets, acoustic guitars, and other stringed instruments; full orchestras, and choirs. Parts of every performance explode as dancers in swirling skirts and silver studded jackets and trousers, tap heels and clap hands. The dancers are very skilled. Sometimes they dance barefoot, wearing shells or other ornaments on their legs to accent rhythm. Other times they wear heeled shoes to dance rapidly on their toes and heels. Sometimes they wear long heavily jeweled robes. They may also dance on stilts, wear masks, or balance tall headdresses on their heads. Female dancers twist and turn their huge full skirts with their hands.

Amalia researched and choreographed over seventy dances. She created and directed an internationally recognized dance company. As a dancer, she performed into her fifties. Standing five feet five inches tall with black hair and fiery dark eyes, Amalia was passionate, determined, and expected perfection. Speaking Spanish and English well, she also had a sense of humor. When others copied her dances and called their groups Ballet Folklórico, she was pleased. However, she renamed her company Ballet Folklórico de México de Amalia Hernández®. That way people knew there was only one with that name.

Family supported Amalia. Her three children danced in the company. Her brother designed the company school with three studios, a theater, and a large foyer for receptions. Her sister created costumes. After Amalia's death, one daughter directed the company and the other managed the school. Her grandson became general manager of the several hundred employees including dancers, musicians, designers, and teachers.

Some people criticize Amalia's dances. They say they are not authentic because she added steps to make them fancier to entertain audiences. But everyone agrees that Amalia's dances show Mexico as a colorful exciting place.

# Create A Dance

Amalia Hernández traveled all over Mexico seeking clues to create her folk dances. She visited tropical forests, flat deserts, high mountains, and coastal plains to observe people living their daily lives.

## *"Folk Dance"*
### Warm Up

- Create a place for your folk dance to show people living their daily lives.

    Is it in the mountains, valleys, close to a river?

    Is it cold or hot?

    What do the people do every day? Work, hunt, fish, go to school?

    What events do they celebrate? Birthdays, weddings, war?

- Decide the purpose for your dance.

    Is it asking for something, celebrating something, or describing something?

    Is it happy, sad, angry, frightening, proud?

- Describe your dance's space, time, energy.

    Are dancers moving in lines or circles?

    Will they stand, kneel, sit, or lie down?

    Are the movements fast or slow?

    Are the movements strong or weak?

    Are they sudden or sustained?

- Name your dance.
- Create three different movements to show the purpose of your dance and its feeling.

### The Dance

- Create a beginning and ending frozen (still) shape or pose for your dance.
- Perform your dance.

## What do you think Amalia would add to your dance?

# Arthur Mitchell
## 1934 -

As a young boy, Arthur Mitchell embraced challenges. With a huge smile and determined attitude, he always gave his full effort. He led "African-American and other racially diverse dancers" onto stages where they had never danced before. Arthur was born in 1934 in Harlem, a large neighborhood in the northern section of New York City. Before 1900 Harlem had been an exclusive white people's neighborhood. However, real estate values changed and they left. Black people migrating from the south moved in and Harlem became one of the most concentrated areas of African-American populations in New York City.

# Reaching Beyond the Norm

In the 1920s and 30s writers, poets, musicians, actors, and artists residing in Harlem created the Harlem Renaissance, a time of artistic expression. Theater companies, popular ballrooms, night clubs, and restaurants thrived. Most of the performers were black, but patrons were both black and white. The music was jazz and the dancing followed syncopated propelling rhythms. Every night hundreds of people flocked to the Savoy Ballroom where black and white people danced together. The Lindy Hop and other forms of jitterbug dancing were the rage.

Arthur was born in the midst of the Great Depression in the United States. Harlem had high unemployment, but the Harlem Renaissance was still evident. Growing up, Arthur liked performing. He was always singing and dancing even when he

helped his father around the apartment building he managed. In fact whenever his family had visitors Arthur put on a show. One of his favorite pastimes was sneaking into nightclubs to watch the hoofers dance.

BORN: March 27, 1934 in Harlem, New York City, United States

But when Arthur was twelve years old his father left. As the oldest son of six children, Arthur had to help support his family. He shined shoes, sold newspapers, delivered meat for a local butcher, and ran errands. He was a smart sharp street kid. He was also very aware of his skin color. He and his friends chanted, "If you're white, you're all right. If you're brown, you may stick around. If you're black, stay back."

One day Arthur's junior high school counselor saw him dancing and encouraged him to audition at New York City's High School of Performing Arts. It had just opened in 1948, and students studied music, drama, and dance along with academic subjects. A neighbor taught Arthur a tap dance. He rented a top hat, white tie and tails, and sang *Steppin' Out with My Baby* for his audition.

Traveling downtown for the audition took courage. Especially since the other applicants had years of training in music, dance, and drama. However, the judges chose Arthur. They liked his nerve, his natural ability, and nice looks. (He was slim and about five feet ten inches tall.) Arthur took dance classes every day, and graduated in 1952 with honors. He thought he would perform in musicals or modern dance. But Lincoln Kirstein, general director of the New York City Ballet, saw Arthur dance and offered him a scholarship to the company's School of American Ballet.

Kirstein, born into a wealthy Boston family, was seventeen years old when he saw his first ballet performance, the Ballets Russes. Liking what he saw, Kirstein visited Europe every year to see the company perform.

 Serge Diaghilev, seen in painting, a Russian businessman and lover of the arts, created Ballets Russes in 1909 to show Russian art and ballet to the world. He encouraged his choreographers and artists to create new ballets and new ways of dancing. Anna Pavlova and Michel Fokine were two of many Russian dancers who performed with Diaghilev.

Kirstein especially liked the work of the young choreographer, George Balanchine, who had graduated from the Russian Imperial Ballet School several years after Anna Pavlova. In 1933 Kirstein convinced Balanchine to join him in forming an American ballet company.

The School of American Ballet began training dancers in 1934. But it took fourteen years and several attempts before a lasting American ballet company would be formed. In 1948 a third company attempt was named Ballet Society. New York City Center invited Ballet Society to become a resident company in its auditorium if it changed its name to the New York City Ballet.

Briefly under the czars Russia had been the world center of classical ballet. With the overturning of the czars in 1917, many dancers left Russia to dance with companies like Ballets Russes. Over time those dancers established ballet companies in other places including England, various European cities, and the United States. By late twentieth century, people recognized New York City as a world center of ballet, and the New York City Ballet as a major company.

The New York City Ballet differed from classical ballet companies in Russia.

First, there were no prima ballerinas. Dancers' names were listed alphabetically as principle dancers, soloists, and corps de ballet.

Second, Russian classical ballets like *The Sleeping Beauty* and *Swan Lake* told familiar stories in four acts as a full evening performance. New York City Ballet presented three or four different dances each performance, and they might not tell a specific story.

Third, Russian classical ballets had beautiful costumes and scenery filling the stage. New York City Ballet dancers often performed in leotards and tights, and danced on empty stages surrounded by black curtains and a white backdrop lit with colored stage lights.

Balanchine, seen in photograph, was the principal choreographer for the company. His style was called neoclassical (new classical). He used classical steps that were centuries old, but he adapted them. For example sometimes he used "off centeredness" and "pelvic and chest movements" instead of keeping the spine erect. He used "angular arms" as well as rounded arms. He also used "turned-in-legs" along with turned out legs.

Additionally he liked jazz rhythms and modern music, and frequently collaborated with the Russian born composer Igor Stravinsky. Often Balanchine based his choreography on the music for the dance instead of a story. His dancers became known for their speed and variations in musical timing.

Through the 1950s in the United States there was bias against black dancers performing ballet. The American Negro Ballet Company in the late 1930s had failed. The black ballerina, Janet Collins, had been hired by the Metropolitan Opera in 1949, but she was an exception. So when Kirstein offered Arthur a scholarship in 1952 he said, "Look Arthur, you're a Negro. If I take you, you've got to be better than anyone else. You've got to work. Will you accept it on those terms?"

Always open to new things, Arthur accepted Kirstein's challenge. He had taken some ballet classes, but forcing his body to train full time at age eighteen was not easy. (Most classical ballet students begin serious training when they are about ten years of age.) However, Arthur was persistent and disciplined. After three years in 1955, Balanchine invited him to join the New York City Ballet. Arthur became the first African American to earn a contract with a major ballet company, just a few years after Jackie Robinson had broken the color barrier in professional baseball.

There were rough times. At Arthur's first performance the audience was totally shocked to see a black dancer. Someone gasped, "Look. They've got a..." and others yelled back, "Give him a chance." However Arthur kept working and was soon dancing leading roles created especially for him. Arthur traveled the world with the New York City Ballet, yet he could not appear with the company on television. As late as 1965 some television stations in the United States refused to show black and white dancers dancing together.

But through his accomplishments, Arthur, seen above, demonstrated that African Americans can excel in classical ballet. He also learned that dance can cut through racial barriers. He said, "As a kid I was up against what every Negro kid is up against, the widespread attitude that if you're not white, blond, or have blue eyes, you're not part of things. But I do believe the arts, especially the dance where you don't have to verbalize, can and will cut through barriers."

Life changed in 1968. In the middle of the civil rights movement in the United States, its leader Dr. Martin Luther King, Jr. was assassinated. Arthur realized that he wanted to do more. So at the top of his own career he stopped performing. He would create a ballet school and company in Harlem, his home neighborhood. Arthur never married.

After the Great Depression and World War II, continued unemployment, poverty, and crime had overtaken Harlem. When Arthur opened his school in 1969, the neighborhood was a haven for selling drugs. Gangs controlled the streets. Half of all children had only one parent or no parents at all. Arthur wanted to help these young people "aspire to something" and "through art to get pride and discipline" and to understand "learning is a pleasure, not a chore".

Arthur put his life savings into the school. With one of his mentors, Karel Shook as co-founder, classes began for thirty students in a deserted garage. Soon four hundred students were registered. Classes included classical ballet, modern, tap, jazz, African and Caribbean dance; music; costume design and stagecraft. Neighborhood residents were always welcome to watch rehearsals.

Just two years later in 1971 Dance Theatre of Harlem gave its first New York City performance. During the next forty plus years it gained recognition as a first class ballet company. It performed throughout the United States, Europe, Australia, Russia, China, Egypt, and South Africa, and earned many medals and citations.

Arthur was surprised that he had to spend so much of his time raising money to keep the company going. Ticket sales alone cannot pay the salaries of all the dancers and staff. When ballet first began in France and Russia the wealth of kings and czars supported it. When governments changed, outside patrons were needed. Finding money was Diaghilev's job when he started Ballet Russes. It was also Kirstein's responsibility when the School of American Ballet began. In 1965 the United States government created the National Endowment for the Arts to help support arts groups. The Ford Foundation also helped fund both the School of American Ballet and the Dance Theatre of Harlem.

As a principal dancer with the New York City Ballet for fifteen years and then by founding Dance Theatre of Harlem, Arthur paved the way for African Americans to perform with classical ballet companies. His school serves several thousand students each year, about half are on scholarship.

◆◆◆

## Create A Dance

Arthur Mitchell identified Dance Theatre of Harlem as a "Classically American" ballet company. As such, several of its ballets have stories with African-American themes.

*Creole Giselle* is a ballet adapted from *Giselle*, the story of a peasant girl whose love is betrayed by a nobleman. The original ballet, created during Marie Taglioni's lifetime and later performed by Anna Pavlova, was placed in Austria. *Creole Giselle* takes place in the United States during the 1830s and 40s. A free black society of sugar plantation owners lived in the Louisiana bayous and they owned slaves. Giselle, a slave, falls in love with the plantation owner, who betrays her. *Creole Giselle* used the original ballet music score composed by Adolph Adam.

Arthur choreographed another story ballet, *John Henry*. It is about the African-American folk hero, John Henry, a steel driver building railroads. When the boss threatens to replace the workers with a steam powered hammer, John Henry tries to prove he can beat the machine. Arthur liked this story, because he said it was what Dance Theatre of Harlem was all about, "those who want to achieve beyond the norm".

## *Hero Dance*

### Warm Up

- Select a folk hero for your dance.
- Decide what your hero wants to do and what obstacles are in the way.
- Select scenes from your hero's life to include in your dance.
- Create three or more movements to show those scenes in your dance.

    Will movements be large, small, strong, weak, fast, slow?

- Describe how your hero feels about the actions.

    Is your hero happy, sad, angry, frightened, proud?

### The Dance

- Select a beginning and ending frozen (still) shape or pose for your dance.
- Perform your dance.

### Can you think of other heroes to dance about?

Dance Theatre of Harlem. Arthur Mitchell performing in *Agon* choreographed by George Balanchine in 1957.

# Illustration Sources
(in book order)

## Chapter 1 - Louis XIV

17th century. *Portrait of Louis XIV and his brother.* Oil on canvas. http://commons.wikimedia.org/
  wiki/File:Portrait_of_King_Louis_XIV_and_his_Brother,_Duc_D%27Orleans.jpg.
1653. *Louis XIV. as Apollo.* http://commons.wikimedia.org/wiki/File:Louis-Apollo1.jpg.
Martin, Pierre-Denis. 1722. *Palace of Versailles.* Versailles Museum, Versailles. http://commons.
  wikimedia.org/wiki/File:Versailles_Pierre-Denis_Martin.jpg.
Isaac. 1721. *Feuillet notation.* In *Dancing by the Book,* by Malkin, Mary Ann O'Brian, Moira Goff,
  Jennifer Thorp, Terry Belanger, and Richard Noble. New York: Privately Printed, 2003.
  http://commons.wikimedia.org/wiki/File:Feuillet_notation.jpg.

## Chapter 2 - John Durang

Willard, Archibald MacNeal. circa 1875. *The Spirit of '76.* Oil on canvas. United States Department
  of State, Washington, DC. http://commons.
  wikimedia.org/wiki/File:Sprit_of_%2776.2.jpeg.
1909. *Stock and horn.* http://commons.wikimedia.org/wiki/File:Stock-and-horn.png.
  In *Grove's Dictionary of Music and Musicians, Volume 4,* 1909 ed., by Pratt, Waldo Selden,
  Charles Newell Boyd, 698. Macmillan, 1909.
Durang, John. n.d. *John Durang in Character of a Hornpipe.* In *The Memoir of John Durang,
  American Actor, 1785-1816,* by Alan S. Downer, ed. Pittsburgh: University of
  Pittsburgh Press for the Historical Society of York County, 1966. From the Collection of
  the York County Heritage Trust, York, PA.

## Chapter 3 - Marie Taglioni

circa 1820. *Filippo Taglioni.* http://en.wikipedia.org/wiki/File:Filippo_Taglioni.jpg.
1845. *Modeplansch ur Stockholms Modejournal.* Photograph. Nordiska Museet, Stockholm. http://
  commons.wikimedia.org/wiki/File:Modeplansch_ur_Stockholms_
  Modejournal,_1845_-_Nordiska_Museet_-_NMA.0032518.jpg.
Arnout, Louis-Jules. circa 1850. *Performance of Meyerbeer's Robert le Diable in the Paris Opera
  House.* Lithograph. http://commons.wikimedia.org/wiki/File:Meyerbeer_
  RobertDiableArnout.jpg.
1832. *Marie Taglioni dancing the title role in "La Sylphide".* http://en.wikipedia.org/wiki/
  File:Sylphide_-Marie_Taglioni_-1832_-2.jpg.

## Chapter 4 - William Henry 'Juba' Lane

Catlin, George. 1827. *Five Points.* Oil on canvas. http://commons.wikimedia.org/wiki/File:Five_
  Points_-_George_Catlin_-_1827.jpg.
Little, Christy. 2014. *Dickens visits Almack's.* Illustration. Based on "Master Juba." *American Notes
  for General Circulation,Volume 1,* by Charles Dickens. Chapman & Hall, 1842. http://
  commons.wikimedia.org/wiki/File:Master_Juba_from_American_Notes.jpg.
1848. *Portrait of Boz's Juba.* http://commons.wikimedia.org/wiki/File:Boz%27s_Juba_portrait.jpg.
Pell's Serenaders. 1848. *Playbill for Pell's Serenaders.* http://commons.wikimedia.org/wiki/
  File:Boz%27s_Juba_announcement,_December_21,_1848.jpg.
1848. "Master Juba." *Illustrated London News.* In *Dan Emmett and the Rise of Early Negro
  Minstrelsy* by Hans Nathan. Norman: University of Oklahoma Press, 1962. http://
  commons.wikimedia.org/wiki/File:Master_Juba.jpg.

## Chapter 5 - Anna Pavlova

1898. *Marius Petipa.* Collection of Adam Lopez. http://commons.wikimedia.org/wiki/
  File:Marius_Ivanovich_Petipa_-Feb._14_1898.JPG.
1891. "Fairy Tale: Students of the Imperial Ballet School." In *Marius Petipa. Materials.
  Recollections. Articles* by Yuri Slonimsky. Leningrad: Leningrad State Theater Museum,
  1971. http://commons.wikimedia.org/wiki/File:Fairy_Tale_-_Students_of_the_
  Imperial_Ballet_School._1891.JPG.
Vardanashvili, Paata. 2007. *Nino Ananiashvili "Swan Lake".* Photograph. http://commons.
  wikimedia.org/wiki/File:Swanlake015.jpg.
Little, Christy. 2014. *Anna and Jack.* Illustration. Based on photograph in *Pavlova: An Illustrated
  Monograph* by Paul Magriel, ed., 49. New York: Henry Holt and Company, 1947.

1905. *Russian ballerina Anna Pavlova as The Dying Swan.* http://commons.wikimedia.org/wiki/
File:AP_Cygne.jpg.

Imperial Mariinsky Theatre. 1898. *Mikhail Fokine, costumed for the role of Lucien d'Hervilly, in
Marius Petipa's production of the ballet Paquita.* In *Nijinsky* by Vera Krasovskaya. Schirmer
Books, 1979. http://commons.wikimedia.org/wiki/File:Paquita_-
Lucien_d%27Hervilly_-Mikhail_Fokine_-circa_1905.JPG.

## Chapter 6 - Rudolf Laban

1882. *Laban aged 3.* Photographer possibly Othmar v. Furk, K. K. Hofphotograph,
Vienna. Reproduction by permission of the Laban Library and Archive.

n.d. *Rudolf Jean Baptiste Attila Laban de Varalja.* In *Living Architecture: Rudolf Laban
and the Geometry of Dance* by Carlisle, Anna, & Valerie Preston-Dunlop.
DVD. 2008. http://commons.wikimedia.org/wiki/File:Rudolf_Laban.png.

circa 1920. *Rudolf Laban as Der Mathematicus (The Mathematician).*
Choreographer Rudolf Laban. Photographer unknown. Reproduction
by permission of the Laban Library and Archive.

circa 1929. *Rudolf von Laban and his Labanotation signs.* In *Rozpravy
Aventina,* 4(36), 358. 1928-1929. Digitized by Czech Academy
of Sciences. http://commons.wikimedia.org/wiki/File:Labanotation1.jpg.

## Chapter 7 - Doris Humphrey

Little, Christy. 2014. *Palace Hotel.* Illustration. Based on illustration from
the Collection of Charles Humphrey Woodford.

Humphrey, Horace. circa 1903. *Doris and White Paws.* Photograph. Collection of
Charles Humphrey Woodford.

Bain News Service. n.d. *Ruth St. Denis.* Library of Congress Prints and Photographs Division,
Washington, D.C. http://commons.wikimedia.org/wiki/File:Ruthstdenis1.jpg.

Green, Lionel. circa 1935. *Doris Humphrey at Bennington.* Photograph. American
Dance Festival Archives.

Humphrey, Horace. n.d. *Tiger.* Photograph. Collection of Charles Humphrey Woodford.

## Chapter 8 - Michio Ito

Little, Christy. 2014. *Playing baseball.* Illustration. Based on photograph from Senda Koreya
Archives. Tsubouchi Memorial Theatre Museum at Waseda University, Tokyo.

Kunisada, Utagawa II. 1865. *Nakamura Nakazo III, Nakamura Kanzaburo XIII, and Ichikawa
Yaozo VI.* http://commons.wikimedia.org/wiki/File:Nakamura_Nakazo_III,_
Nakamura_Kanzaburo_XIII_and_Ichikawa_Yaozo_VI_%281865%29.jpg.

1912. *Sailing to Marseilles.* Photographer unknown. Ito Family Collection.

1912. *Emile Jaques-Dalcroze.* Photograph. In *E. Jaques-Dalcroze: Seine Stellung und Aufgabe in
unserer Zeit Stuttgart* by Storck, Karl. Stuttgart: Greiner und Pfeiffer, 1912. http://
commons.wikimedia.org/wiki/File:Emile_Jaques_Dalcroze.jpg.

Genthe, Arnold. 1919. "Michio Itō." *Shadowland, Sep 1919-Feb 1920,* 13. http://commons.
wikimedia.org/wiki/File:Michio_Ito_4_-_Nov_1919_Shadowland.jpg.

Miyatake, Toyo. 1929. *Michio Ito in "Pizzicati".* Choreographer Michio Ito. Photograph.
Permission Toyo Miyatake Studio. San Gabriel.CA.

## Chapter 9 - Mrinalini Sarabhai

n.d. *As young girl.* Courtesy, Mrinalini Sarabhai, Darpana, Ahmedabad.

1940. *Rukmini Devi Arundale.* http://commons.wikimedia.org/wiki/File:Rukmini_Devi.jpg.

1965. Courtesy, Mrinalini Sarabhai, Darpana, Ahmedabad.

1955. Courtesy, Mrinalini Sarabhai, Darpana, Ahmedabad.

circa 1940. *Rabindranath Tagore reading* http://commons.wikimedia.org/wiki
File:Rabindranath_Tagore_reading.jpg.

## Chapter 10 - Pearl Primus

circa 1939. *Young Pearl*. Photographer unknown. American Dance Festival Archives.

Darby, Eileen. n.d. *Asadata Dafora*. Photograph. Jacob's Pillow Dance Festival Archives.

Peterich, Gerda. 1943. *Pearl Primus in "The Negro Speaks of Rivers"*. Choreographer Pearl Primus. Photograph. Milne Special Collections and Archives Department, University of New Hampshire Library, Durham, NH. American Dance Festival Archives.

Jordan, Leon M. 1952. *Pearl as anthropologist in Liberia*. Photograph. Leon M. Jordan Collection. Used by permission of the University of Missouri-Kansas City Libraries, Dr. Kenneth J. LaBudde Department of Special Collections.

## Chapter 11 - Amalia Hernández

n.d. *Aztec Warriors*. Foundation for the Advancement of Mesoamerican Studies, Inc. http://commons.wikimedia.org/wiki/File:Codex_Mendoza_folio_67r_bottom.jpg.

n.d. *Zapatista Women*. http://commons.wikimedia.org/wiki/File:Zapatistawomen.png.

Vechten, Carl Van. 1940. *Portrait of Argentinita*. Photograph. Library of Congress Prints and Photographs Division, Washington, D.C. http://commons.wikimedia.org/wiki/File:La_Argentinita.tif.

Miyatake, Toyo. 1932. *Waldeen*. Photograph. Permission Toyo Miyatake Studio, San Gabriel, CA.

## Chapter 12 - Arthur Mitchell

Bakst, Leon. 1906. *Portrait of Serge Diaghilev and His Nanny*. Oil on canvas. http://commons.wikimedia.org/wiki/File:Bakst_daighilev.jpg.

LeClerq, Tanaquil. n.d. *George Balanchine*. Photograph. NYCB Archives Tanaquil LeClerq Collection, New York City. http://commons.wikimedia.org/wiki/File:George_Balanchine_portrait_taken_by_Tanaquil_LeClerq.jpg.

Vechten, Carl Van. 1955. *Portrait of Arthur Mitchell*. Photograph. Library of Congress Prints and Photographs Division, Washington, D.C. http://commons.wikimedia.org/wiki/File:Arthur_Mitchell.jpg.

2007. *Dance Theatre of Harlem*. Photograph. http://commons.wikimedia.org/wiki/File:Dancetheatre.jpg.

# General Resources

Au, Susan. 2002. *Ballet and Modern Dance*. 2nd ed. Thames and Hudson.
Beaumont, Cyril W. 1938. *Complete Book of Ballets*. New York: Grosset & Dunlap.
De Mille, Agnes. 1963. *The Book of the Dance*. New York: Golden Press, Inc.
Dunkin, Anne. 2006. *Dancing in Your School: A Guide for Preschool and
      Elementary School Teachers*. Hightstown: Princeton Book Company.
Emery, Lynne Fauley. 1988. *Black Dance from 1619 to Today*.
      2nd rev. ed. Hightstown: Princeton Book Company.
Kirstein, Lincoln. 1984. *Four Centuries of Ballet: Fifty
      Masterworks*. Mineola: Dover Publications, Inc.
Kraus, Richard, Sarah Chapman Hilsendager, and Brenda Dixon. 1991. *History
      of the Dance in Art and Education*. Upper Saddle River: Prentice Hall, Inc.
Needham, Maureen, ed. 2002. *I See America Dancing: Selected Readings
      1685-2000*. Champaign: University of Illinois Press.
Perpener, John O. III. 2005. *African-American Concert Dance: The Harlem
      Renaissance and Beyond*. Champaign: University of Illinois Press.
Stearns, Marshall, and Jean Stearns. 1968. *Jazz Dance: The Story of
      American Vernacular Dance*. New York: The Macmillan Company.
Zimmer, Elizabeth. 1983. *Dancing in the Americas: A Dance
      History Resource Guide*. New York: ArtsConnection.

# Subject Specific Sources and Endnotes

## Chapter 1 - Louis XIV

Brandenberg, Aliki. 1989. *The King's Day: Louis XIV of France*. New York: Thomas Y. Crowell.
Hilton, Wendy. 1981. *Dance of Court and Theater: The French Noble Style 1690-1725*.
      Hightstown: Princeton Book Company.

## Chapter 2 - John Durang

Downer, Alan S., ed. 1966. *The Memoir of John Durang: American Actor 1785-1816*. Pittsburgh:
      University of Pittsburgh Press for the Historical Society of York County.
John Durang Puppet Theatre Museum at the Hole in the Wall Puppet Theatre,
      Lancaster, Pennsylvania. www.holeinthewallpuppet.com.

### Endnotes

"Twenty-two steps" of Durang's Hornpipe. Stearns, 38.

## Chapter 3 - Marie Taglioni

Looseleaf, Victoria. 2007. "The Story of the Tutu: Ballet's Signature Costume Has A Fabled
      Past and A Glamorous Present." *Dance Magazine* 81(10): 52-54, 56.

### Endnotes

"This little ugly duckling . . . dance." De Mille, 105. Original read 'little hunchback'.
"Taglioni floats . . . bending them." De Mille, 105-106.

## Chapter 4 - William Henry 'Juba' Lane

Cook, James W. 2003. "Dancing Across the Color Line." *Common-place:
      The Interactive Journal of Early American Life, Inc.* 4(1).
Johnson, Stephen. 2003. "Juba's Dance: An Assessment of Newly Acquired Information."
      *Proceedings of the 26th Annual Conference of the Society for Dance History Scholars*.

### Endnotes

" . . . snapping his fingers . . . no legs." From Charles Dickens' *American Notes for
      General Circulation, Vol.1*. London: Oxford, 1957. pp90-1. Johnson, 8.
"Juba this... Juba that..." Stearns, 27-29.
"The dancing of Juba . . . Europe." Johnson, 10.
"Rhythm Story Dance". Dunkin, 95.

## Chapter 5 - Anna Pavlova

Allman, Barbara. 2001. *The Dance of the Swan: A Story about Anna Pavlova.*
    Minneapolis: Carolrhoda Books, Inc.
Magriel, Paul, ed. 1947. *Pavlova: An Illustrated Monograph.* New York: Henry Holt and Company.

### Endnotes

"One day . . . very theater." Magriel, 2.
"She danced . . . tip of her toe." Beaumont, 640.

## Chapter 6 - Rudolf Laban

Bradley, Karen, email correspondence, June 30, 2008.
Guest, Ann Hutchinson, personal interview, June 25, 2008.
Laban, Rudolf. 1975. *A Life for Dance: Reminiscences.* Translated and annotated by Lisa Ullmann.
    New York: Theatre Arts Books.

## Chapter 7 - Doris Humphrey

Cohen, Selma Jeanne. 1972. *Doris Humphrey, An Artist First.* Hightstown:
    Princeton Book Company.
Humphrey, Doris. 1959. *The Art of Making Dances.* New York: Holt, Rinehart and Winston.
Stodelle, Ernestine. n.d. "Steel and Velvet: A Centennial Reminiscence." *The Doris Humphrey*
    *Society.* Accessed June 6, 2014. http://www.dorishumphrey. org/steel-velvet.
Woodford, Charles Humphrey, personal interview, June 22, 2007.

### Endnotes

"How can... like that." Cohen, 14.
"missionary work". Woodford.
"was a shaft... stage"... "steel and velvet". Stodelle.

## Chapter 8 - Michio Ito

Breslauer, Jan. "New Legs for a Legend: He wowed 'em at the Bowl, pioneered modern dance—
    but did you ever hear of Michio Ito?" *Los Angeles Times,* Calendar, March 15, 1998: 7, 84.
Cowell, Mary-Jean. 1994. "East and West in the Work of Michio Ito."
    *Dance Research Journal* 26(2): 11-23.
————, personal conversation, June 26, 2008.
————, email correspondence, March 2, 2009; April 21, 2014.
Ito, Michele, email correspondence, January 23, 2009.
Takeishi, Midori. 2006. *Japanese Elements in Michio Ito's Early Period (1915-1924): Meeting*
    *of East and West in the Collaborative Works.* Edited by David Edward Pacun.
    Tokyo: Gendaitosho.
————, email correspondence, June 9, 2009.

### Endnotes

"Do the impossible." Takeishi, 7.
"modern boy". Cowell, 2008.
"My teaching embraces . . . control of all three." Cowell, 1994:14.
"In my dancing . . . only myself." ibid., 11.

## Chapter 9 - Mrinalini Sarabhai

Bhavnani, Enakshi. 1965. *The Dance in India.* Bombay: D.B. Taraporevala Sons & Co. Private Ltd.
Sarabhai, Mrinalini. 2004. *The Voice of the Heart.* New Delhi: Harpers Collins Publishers India.

### Endnotes

"I am a dancer." Sarabhai, introduction.

## Chapter 10 - Pearl Primus

Martin, John. Dance Review. *The New York Times*. February, 21, 1943.

Schwartz, Peggy, and Murray Schwartz. 2011. *The Dance Claimed Me: A Biography of Pearl Primus*. New Haven: Yale University Press.

————, telephone interview, September 18, 2012.

————, correspondence, October 13, 2012.

### Endnotes

"Earth Dancer" as self identification. Schwartz correspondence, 2012.

"a remarkably gifted artist . . . and the freedom to do what she chooses with it." Martin.

"bewildered and numb" . . . "poverty" . . . "intensity of the hatred and fear" . . . "both black and white". Schwartz, 46.

"regal, majestic". Schwartz phone interview, 2012.

"soaring high leaps". Schwartz, 95.

"strength of a panther". ibid., 30.

"the walk and all its variations . . . to the ground". Stearns, 12-13.

"hugging the earth". Schwartz, 76.

## Chapter 11 - Amalia Hernández

Looseleaf, Victoria. "Carrying on a Mother's Spirited Work." *Los Angeles Times*, Calendar, September 16, 2001: 54-55.

Rankin, Allen. 1963. "Born to Dance." *Readers Digest* 83(493): 234-240.

Shay, Anthony. 2002. *Choreographic Politics: State Folk Dance Companies, Representation, and Power*. Middletown: Wesleyan University Press.

————, email correspondence, September 22, 2010; September 24, 2010.

University Musical Society. 2006. UMS Youth Education 06/07 *Amalia Hernández Ballet Folkorico de México Teacher Resource Guide*. Ann Arbor: UMS Youth Education Program.

### Endnotes

"you may learn to dance . . . for me and your uncles." Rankin, 235.

"Folk Dance". Dunkin, 101.

## Chapter 12 - Arthur Mitchell

1989. *Dance Theater of Harlem*. 120 min. Videorecording. Produced by RM Arts/Danmarks Radio Co-production. Public Media Home Vision.

Estrada, Ric. 1968. "3 Leading Negro Artists, and how they feel about dance in the community." *Dance Magazine* 42(11): 45-60.

Gottschild, Brenda Dixon. 2004 "Balanchine in Black." *Dance Magazine,* October: 99-101.

Levine, Debra. "Talking with Dance Theatre of Harlem's Co-Founder Arthur Mitchell." *Los Angeles Times*, Calendar. July 6, 2010.

Taylor, Burton. "How the Creole 'Giselle' Took Form." *The New York Times*, October 14, 1984.

Judy Tyrus, email correspondence, December 28, 2012.

### Endnotes

"African-American and other racially diverse". www.dancetheatreofharlem.org. Accessed June 20, 2014.

"If you're white . . . stay back." Emery, 280.

"off centeredness" . . . "pelvic and chest movements" . . . "angular arms" . . . "turned in legs". Gottschild, 100.

"Look Arthur . . . accept it on those terms?" Estrada, 52.

"Look. They've got . . . chance." Levine.

"As a kid... barriers." *Dance Theater of Harlem* videorecording.

"aspire to something" . . . "through art . . . discipline" . . . "learning . . . chore". ibid.

"Classically American". Tyrus.

"those . . . norm". *Dance Theater of Harlem* videorecording.

# Index

# About The Author

Anne Dunkin has always danced! She performed with the Washington Ballet, Ballet Cirque, and the Ethel Butler Dance Company before co-founding her own company, Qwindo's Window, with Brad Willis. Introducing dance to hundreds of thousands of young people, the company toured throughout the Eastern/Midwestern United States for twelve years performing and providing classroom workshops. Locations included public school all-purpose rooms; early childhood, migrant, and special education centers; CAMI Hall and on the streets of Harlem in New York City, and residencies at the JFK Center for the Performing Arts and the Smithsonian Institution in Washington, DC.

As a dance educator in the private sector, Anne established dance studios in suburban Washington, DC and Los Angeles, CA and was Assistant Director at Raoul Gelabert's Studio in New York City. She created the syllabus, *First Steps First*, and conducted seminars presenting creative movement as age-appropriate dance instruction for young dancers three to six years old. Additionally she published articles in *Dance Teacher Now* providing reasons and methods for including all students in private sector dance classes and introducing arts education and anatomical considerations. She also taught dance at Kendall Demonstration Elementary School at Gallaudet College for the deaf in Washington, DC, at Gill St. Bernard's K-12 private school in Bernardsville, New Jersey, and at Landmark West School for students with language based learning differences in Encino, California.

Advocating PreK-12 dance education, Anne taught "teaching dance" to pre-service teachers at California State University, Fullerton for ten years. Her book, *Dancing in Your School: A Guide for Preschool and Elementary School Teachers*, was published by Princeton Book Company in 2006. She earned an M.A. in Human Development Education from the University of Maryland, College Park, and her Ph.D. from the University of California, Riverside, is in Dance History and Theory. She currently coordinates the *Dance Education Literature and Research descriptive index*, an online archive, for the National Dance Education Organization.

CPSIA information can be obtained
at www.ICGtesting.com
Printed in the USA
LVHW020055211221
706819LV00006B/283

9 780997 713503